Victorian Scotland

James Crawford, Lesley Ferguson and Kristina Watson

Victorian Scotland

Royal Commission on the
Ancient and Historical Monuments
of Scotland

HER MOST GRACIOUS MAJESTY QUEEN VICTORIA in the 60th YEAR of her Reign

Introduction

It was an age of cities and slums, socialism and evolution, empire and tourism, poverty and democracy. It was the greatest period of progress the world had ever seen. Change was a constant. Contradiction was a constant. It was *not* the best of times. It was *not* the worst of times. But it was the era that made us who we are today.

The Victorians' relentless pursuit of progress was matched by their passion for consumption and their love of bigger and better. The nineteenth century was filled to the brim with sensations – many of them new and never before seen – as whole cityscapes rose in a clamour of noise, smoke, steam and people. Yet in the midst of all that upheaval and turmoil, surrounded by the dizzying pace of a society that felt it could always go faster, were individuals framed by stillness, manipulating devices that fundamentally changed how they saw themselves and how they saw everything around them. These were the world's first photographers.

In 1841, William Henry Fox Talbot, an English scientist and artist, patented a process that would form the basis for all modern photography. After years of experimentation, he had at last captured "the inimitable beauty of the pictures of Nature's painting … fairy pictures, creations of a moment". Of all the great Victorian inventions, none excited the popular imagination quite like the photograph. Over the next half-century, a whole range of forms, techniques and equipment was developed, culminating in what the era did best – the industrialisation of photography. In 1888, George Eastman's No. 1 Kodak Camera was launched with the simple slogan "You press the button, we do the rest." The camera and the photograph had reached the apex of mass-production: a medium that had once been the province of the privileged few was open to everyone. As the art critic Lady Elizabeth Eastlake had foreseen in a famous essay in *The Quarterly Review* in 1857, photography had become "a household word and a household want; it is used alike by art and science, by love, business, and justice; is found in the most sumptuous saloon, and in the dingiest attic – in the solitude of the Highland cottage and in the glare of the London gin-palace – in the pocket of the detective, in the cell of the convict, in the folio of the painter and architect, among the papers and patterns of the mill-owner and manufacturer, and on the cold brave breast on the battlefield".

In the National Collection of the Royal Commission on the Ancient and Historical Monuments of Scotland, many diverse fragments of this Victorian photographic phenomenon are brought together. In images of grand construction works in emerging cities, in records of engineering miracles like the Forth Bridge, in depictions of romantic Highland landscapes in the first ever tourist albums, and in rare shots of slum clearances, the narrative emerges of a nation in the middle of a great transformation – its people both fascinated and bewildered by the changing world around them. The impact of these preserved moments – now over a century distant – is undiminished. With our modern eyes we see what is lost, we know what is different, we recognise what remains. But, most of all, we share the wide-eyed wonder of the Victorian pioneers – the men and women who first stared through a camera lens, opened and closed a shutter, and captured Scotland in a photograph.

Queen Victoria was the first monarch in history to be more photographed than painted. This portrait comes from a supplement to the *Lady's Pictorial* in 1897, held in an album compiled by Miss Lizzie M Murray at Woodside House, Perthshire.
GUNN & STUART PHOTOGRAPHERS
1897 DP074534

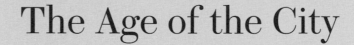

The Age of the City

In February 1875, Richard Cross, Home Secretary of Benjamin Disraeli's recently appointed government, presented to the House of Commons a new Bill designed to tackle the inhuman slums plaguing Victorian cities. As he neared the end of his speech, Cross issued a rallying cry to the civic authorities of Britain, "I ask you on these dens of wretchedness and misery to cast one ray of hope and happiness; I ask you on these haunts of sickness and of death to breathe, at all events, one breath of health and life; and on these courts and alleys where all is dark with a darkness which not only may be, but is felt – a darkness of mind, body and soul – I ask you to assist in carrying out one of God's best and earliest laws, – 'Let there be light'".

Ten years before these emotive words filled the House, the councillors of Glasgow had already looked on with horror at their city's heart of darkness. Poverty, filth, pollution, overcrowding, disease and degradation had overcome the Old Town, imprisoning more than 50,000 of the most unfortunate working classes in 80 acres of stygian courts and closes where typhus and cholera roamed free. "No person of common humanity", declared Friedrich Engels, "would stable a horse" in such conditions.

The city authorities knew something had to be done, but they did not know what. When reports reached them of Baron George-Eugene Haussmann's ambitious redesign of central Paris, a deputation of Glasgow city elders, including the Lord Provost, the Medical Officer of Health and the City Architect John Carrick, set off on a fact-finding mission to the French capital. What greeted them was a city reborn. The medieval fabric of central Paris had been almost completely demolished, and in its place the visitors wandered a sparkling layout of wide boulevards, circuses, and broad public spaces. Transfixed by Haussmann's 'miracle', they returned to Clydeside with a radical vision for a new Glasgow.

The Glasgow City Improvement Act of 1866 began a programme of work on a scale never before seen in a British city. The ulcerous slums around Gallowgate, Trongate, Saltmarket and Glasgow Cross were swept away, 39 new streets were created, existing ones were widened and realigned, and whole blocks were rebuilt, led by Carrick's imposition of a unitary style, with guidelines for street widths, building heights and even architectural idiom. The incredible scale of the experiment resonated throughout Victorian Britain – and in particular reached Disraeli's new administration. It was Glasgow's remarkable transformation that provided the cue for the Home Secretary's luminous, biblical instruction to the nation's civic planners.

This need to light the dark of the Victorian city had been growing ever more desperate as the nineteenth century progressed. Britain was the world's first industrialised urban society. It gave birth to the modern factory city, and the child was trouble from the start: dirty, ill and wretched, yet at the same time bloated,

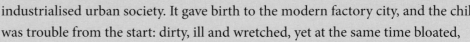

greedy and ruthless. Contrasts abounded, the result of an incredible con-
glomeration of people, commerce, traffic, squalor, wealth, misery and noise.
The Victorian city was at once Babylon and Hades, a brave new world and the
end of civilisation. The gothic spires of imperialist architecture pointed to the
heavens, while the steeple chimneys of the mills and factories produced a dark,
fiery smoke that eclipsed the sky and seemed to be drawn from hell itself.

The Victorians were firm believers that building design reflected the
cultural sentiments of the age. The health of a people and its civilisation could
be traced in its streets, houses, churches, halls and monuments. As cityscapes
careered out of control at an incredible pace, driven on by the clanging metro-
nome of the industrial machine, they faced the reality that, behind the grand
facades built by an unprecedented civic wealth, the faceless utilitarian bulk
of innumerable factories – and the shapeless, jerry-built misery of workers'
quarters – revealed a society in desperate need of salvation.

The architecture of cities became a battleground for the Victorian soul.
What claims could they make of progress, and what would be their legacy,
if the metropolis of the nineteenth century was an organ grinder of human
suffering, an environment that debased its citizens and forced them into an
urban savagery? The deliberately classical or gothic buildings that came to
dominate Victorian cities, from Glasgow's Royal Exchange to Edinburgh's Scott
Monument, were stone statements of rectitude, an attempt through architecture to create the reassuring morality of an idealised past in the midst of a
terrifying new world of dissolute industrialism.

Along with Glasgow's revolutionary programme of urban renewal, these
architectural bids to win civic hearts and minds marked a starting point,
not an end. The Victorian era set the riddle of the modern city. Among such
a crush of people, why was alienation and loneliness the common experience? As more and more workers stepped on to the industrial treadmill, how
could they be elevated above the status of insignificant cogs in the immense
machine? And could proud, evocative architecture really help to repair the
crumbling bonds of brotherhood and community?

The new age of the city had begun.

Looking from Princes Street over
Canal Street Station – now Waverley
Station – a crowded mass of buildings
jostles for position along the medieval
spine of Edinburgh's Old Town. In 1847,
Hans Christian Andersen described the
unsavoury sights at the heart of the old city,
"many streets off it are narrow, filthy and
with six-storey houses; one has to think of
the great buildings in the dirty towns of
Italy; poverty and misery seem to peep
out of the open hatches which normally
serve as windows".
JAMES GOOD TUNNY 1854 DP073556

In 1849, George William Bell, a Licentiate of the Royal College of Surgeons of Edinburgh, and the city's first 'examiner' of the registers of births, marriages and deaths, published *Day and Night in the Wynds of Edinburgh*, a pamphlet exposing the squalid conditions prevalent throughout the Old Town. In the course of his work, he wrote he had visited "dens inhabited by outdoor paupers, beggars, vagrants, the parents of ragged school-children … hidden among the masses of rotten, rat-haunted buildings behind the Grassmarket, Cowgate, West Port etc … No description can convey an adequate idea of the horrors of these places." Descriptions may have been as inadequate as Bell said, but there was a growing understanding of the power of photography to record stark representations of poverty. Pictured here are two images from the Edinburgh Improvement Trust survey, showing derelict houses at the east end of College Wynd in the Cowgate.

ARCHIBALD BURNS 1871

SC1107709 & SC1107708

RIGHT

A woman and two children look out from the decaying doorway of Stenhouse grain mill in Edinburgh.

JOHN FLEMING c1890 SC1124541

Seeking to improve the appearance of their urban landscapes, the industrialised cities of Victorian Britain looked back to the models of ancient Greece and Rome, convinced that truly great architecture, art and philosophy flowed first from mercantile, manufacturing and imperial wealth. Glasgow's Royal Exchange Square drew inspiration from Rome's Forum of Augustus, with the building at its centre converted from a Tobacco Lord's mansion and refaced in the early nineteenth century with a huge portico of Corinthian columns. Further extensions in 1880 added a mansard roof, which housed the city's first telephone exchange.

THOMAS ANNAN c1875 SC1075748

Glasgow – The Trongate St –

The 1866 Glasgow City Improvement Act launched the most comprehensive plan of civic improvement in the Victorian era. The Trongate was one of many areas around the city's old, medieval core that were transformed by this ambitious programme of demolition and reconstruction. When Octavia Hill, the famous London housing reformer and co-founder of the National Trust, walked the new streets of Glasgow in 1874 she "found here and there a house, here and there whole sides of a close or alley, had been taken down to let in the brightening influence of sun and air. The haggard, wretched population which usually huddles into dark, out-of-the-way places, was swarming over the vacant ground for years unvisited by sun and wind … I felt as if some bright and purifying angel had laid a mighty finger on the squalid and neglected spot. Those open spaces, those gleams of sunlight, those playing children, seemed earnest of better things to come – of better days in store."

Glasgow – St George's Square –

Originally surrounded by housing with a private, fenced garden at its centre, the arrival of the railway in the mid nineteenth century saw Glasgow's George Square almost completely colonised by hotels. The gardens were replaced with statues of notable Scots, including Robert Burns, Walter Scott and Sir John Moore of Corunna – famous son of Glasgow and a hero of the Peninsular War.

While slums and industry had consumed much of Glasgow's old centre, the wealthy had looked west, building large, honey-coloured mansions in long streets and avenues on the slopes of Blythswood Hill, Yorkhill and Garnethill. Pictured here is architect John Thomas Rochead's Ruskin Terrace. Overlooking the stretch of Great Western Road leading to the Botanic Gardens, it emerged into mid-nineteenth century Glasgow like a grand Italian palazzo. **THOMAS ANNAN c1870** DP074785

Photographer Thomas Annan, famous for his work recording the slums of central Glasgow, creates an almost pastoral scene here in the midst of the workshop of the world, as two well-dressed men stare across a still Clyde to the wide arches of the Jamaica Street Bridge. First built by Thomas Telford in the early nineteenth century, the bridge was reconstructed and widened between 1894 and 1899 as a replica of the original, deliberately retaining Telford's granite facings and balustrades.

THOMAS ANNAN c1880 DP010489

TOP

John Thomas Rochead's future vision for the Wallace Monument is clearly evident here in the strident baronial architecture of this branch of the City of Glasgow Bank, constructed on the corner of the Trongate and Nelson Street in 1854. The Bank became infamous for its spectacular collapse in October 1878, with speculative investments in Australian wool and an unlimited liability structure seeing all but 254 of its 1,200 shareholders ruined.

THOMAS ANNAN c1875 DP074783

ABOVE

Built in 1835 as an unusually wide, mercantile street, by the late nineteenth century, Glasgow's St Vincent Place had become the site for two grand financial institutions – John Thomas Rochead's bold, Italianate Bank of Scotland, and John Burnet's renaissance inspired Clydesdale Bank, seen here on the right of the picture

GEORGE WASHINGTON WILSON c1890
SC1075780

Looking down the wide, airy New Town thoroughfare of Edinburgh's Hanover Street, the photographer captures William Playfair's massive Doric temple of art head on. In light and shadow, the Royal Institution's profusion of carved stone is shown in sharp relief, with the lens of the camera meeting directly the imperious stare of Queen Victoria – depicted as Britannia – on her throne. The contrast between this classical temple and the irregular spires, turrets and chimneys of the Old Town is particularly marked.

GEORGE WASHINGTON WILSON pre1880
DP073936

Can the soul of a city be judged through the character of its monuments? Within weeks of the death of the internationally celebrated novelist and poet Sir Walter Scott, a committee of noblemen was formed to raise subscriptions to create a fitting memorial. An architectural competition saw 54 designs submitted, including

22 gothic structures, 11 ornamental statues, 14 Grecian temples, 5 pillar monuments, an obelisk and a fountain. George Meikle Kemp – entering under the pseudonym John Morvo, the name of the medieval master mason of Melrose Abbey – was the eventual winner. Built between 1840 and 1846, his strikingly

romantic, 200ft tall, gothic tower erupted as if from another age among the ordered, classical architecture of Edinburgh's New Town.
DAVID OCTAVIUS HILL c1845 SC466197
? JAMES GOOD TUNNY c1854 DP073555

CALTON HILL   J PATRICK.

From Calton Hill – with Calton Jail in the foreground – the unique contrasts of the Edinburgh cityscape are clearly visible. The heaped anthill of medieval buildings running down the lee of the Castle Rock faces-off against the rigid geometric blocks and crescents of the Georgian New Town. In Victorian Edinburgh, the urban development of the eighteenth and nineteenth centuries had clearly segregated wealth and poverty, creating one city for the rich, another for the poor.

JOHN PATRICK c1890 SC1120429

From the Castlegate, Aberdeen's market-place from the twelfth century, the facades of a sparkling new nineteenth century city unfurl down the crystalline granite mile of Union Street. The Victorian era saw an explosion in Aberdeen's size and wealth, with local granite from the Rubislaw quarry providing a strong, distinctive building material that came to characterise the shape and appearance of the city. Dominating this photograph are architects Peddie and Kinnear's Town and County Buildings, a typically confident Victorian civic structure that subsumed the old Tolbooth tower and created a new, thrusting gothic tower to stud the Aberdeen skyline.

GEORGE WASHINGTON WILSON pre1880
DP073918

Harry Bedford Lemere was one of the principal architectural photographers of the Victorian era. He travelled throughout Britain, taking pictures of the homes and buildings of the rich, sometimes for the owners, sometimes as a record for professional architects or decorators. Bedford Lemere used natural light rather than flash, which required long exposure times and meant he only very rarely included figures in his photography. Here he captures the hushed ostentation of the telling hall of the British Linen Bank in Edinburgh's St Andrew Square. The evocative impact of the long exposure is clear in this image, as shafts of light from the hall's central dome catch a line of Composite columns of polished Peterhead granite. The Edinburgh Head Office was designed in 1846 by the architect David Bryce, his commission to create a temple of finance on the grandest scale. It was in 1896, to commemorate the 150th anniversary of the founding of the British Linen Company, that Bedford Lemere was hired to photograph the Bank's sumptuous interior.

H BEDFORD LEMERE 1896 SC700912

Land of the Mountain and the Flood

"From shore to shore the whole island is to be set … thick with chimneys: and there shall be no meadows in it; no trees; no gardens; only a little corn grown upon the housetops, reaped and threshed by steam … you do not leave even room for roads, but travel either over the roofs of your mills, on viaducts; or under their floors, in tunnels … The smoke having rendered the light of the sun unserviceable, you work always by the light of your own gas." Writing in 1859, the celebrated English art critic and social thinker John Ruskin summed up – with doom-laden eloquence – a general societal disquiet over the rapid industrial and urban encroachment on Britain's traditional landscapes. Yet, while the muscular tendrils of this gloomy 'factory land' were coming to dominate the Midlands of England, and threatened to turn the central belt of Glasgow and Edinburgh into some great, louring conurbation, for much of Scotland, and in particular the remote reaches of the Highlands, these new urban centres were at most dark smudges on the horizon, rumours and stories, as tangible as hearth smoke. Physical distance had insulated many communities from the rapid advancements of the modern age. But this isolation, often born of long-established self-sufficiency, could not last forever.

The city was more than just a dense concentration of workplaces and housing. It represented a focal point for wealth and government, and generated a powerful gravity greater than its own mass, drawing ever more people and landscapes into its orbit. By the time of Victoria's reign, it was the engine room sustaining the British Empire, and it was also the ultimate consumer, its enormous appetite for food, water, energy – and lives – rarely satisfied. These economic pressures, and the constant quest for resources, turned the city's covetous eye outwards towards what Walter Scott called the "land of the mountain and the flood". For many rural landowners gazing back, the city's burgeoning free market represented an unprecedented commercial opportunity – but an opportunity that could only be realised by modernising lifestyles and landscapes that had persisted for countless generations.

Whether an economic necessity brought on by a rising population and insufficient employment, or an act of greed by the ruling landed class, from the late eighteenth to the late nineteenth century, the desertion or forced eviction of the Highland townships left behind a ghost landscape of crumbling buildings and innumerable grazing sheep. Many of the dispossessed had no option but to try their luck in the cities or overseas in the New World, while others were resettled precariously in crofting communities – marginal lands on holdings too small to be viable economic farms, with no security of tenure. The crofts were intended to provide a measure of subsistence while the remnants of the Highland population learnt to diversify in industries like weaving, kelp or commercial fishery – yet many of these economic initiatives failed, often because of the vast distances between the remote communities and their potential markets, or because they were overtaken and superseded by newer processes. Crofters' frustrations eventually turned violent and after a period of prolonged unrest, which reached a peak when Glasgow police were despatched to enforce an eviction order on Skye and warships were sent to the Minch, the government had to act.

In 1883, Prime Minister William Gladstone established a Royal Commission to "inquire into the condition of the Crofters and Cottars in the Highlands and Islands of Scotland". Its Chairman, Lord Napier, travelled extensively around the northern and western reaches of the country, and was often appalled by the living conditions he found. "His habitation is usually of a character which would almost imply physical and moral degradation in the eyes of those who do not know how much decency, courtesy, virtue, and even mental refinement, survive amidst the sordid surroundings of a Highland hovel." Similar stories were repeated across the regions with the people, "complaining of the smallness of their holding and its inferior quality, of the up-handedness of the factors, and the oppression of the landlords". Vivid pictures taken by photographers like George Washington Wilson bolstered the findings of the Royal Commission, and, when made public, they dispelled forever the sentimental Victorian view of life in the Highland crofting communities. The resulting legislation, the *1886 Crofters' Act*, made clearances illegal and gave the tenants security and the right to bequeath the crofts to their children in the six crofting counties, but it remained a hard, marginal life and the Act did little to stop the population exodus.

Just like the era's new invention of photography, each picture in the Victorian age has its opposite, its negative. While the disenfranchised of the rural communities left their landscapes behind, a new class of working man grown rich from industry was moving in. Grand, gothic houses were built as opulent status symbols, advertisements of achievement that gazed out over acres of manicured parklands. For men like William Arrol, the apprentice blacksmith turned legendary Victorian engineer, or Sir James Mackenzie, the prosperous silk merchant, the country retreat was an essential escape from the city, a reminder that Ruskin's dark, dystopian vision of a nation without countryside had not come true. Except, in some sense, it had. In the space of little more than a century, the dynamic of the rural environment had been completely transformed. From providing a home for the majority of the Scottish population, it had been reinvented as an industrial resource and a commodity – a landscape of beautiful vistas and barren townships, a millionaire's playground and a bottomless well of memories.

PREVIOUS PAGES
Travellers in a horse and trap pause on a country road by Lochearnhead. Although the nineteenth century saw a huge population movement to the towns and cities, Scotland's rapidly expanding urban and industrial environments were in their relative infancy. Early photographers exploring the countryside captured a national landscape still dominated by agricultural labour.
1892 DP071918

RIGHT
A tourist 'snapshot' creates a vision of a rural idyll, with a cottage – possibly at the entrance to Glen Nevis – resting in the shade of an avenue of tall trees.
c1875 DP069247

TOP LEFT
Lady Henrietta Gilmour, a wealthy Renfrewshire aristocrat, took up photography as a hobby after the birth of her seventh child. One of Scotland's earliest women photographers, her work carried the implicit imprint of her social status, recording scenes on her family estate in Fife or – as with these picturesque cottages at Onich – during visits to country houses in the west of Scotland in the sporting season. For much of the century, amateur photography remained an expensive pastime of the wealthy, with the results often presenting a romanticised view of rural life.

LADY HENRIETTA GILMOUR 1899

SC1115559

BOTTOM LEFT
Despite growing prosperity elsewhere in Victorian Scotland, years of starvation, poverty and oppression had taken their toll on crofting communities, as here at Kentangaval on Barra, with many leaving to seek employment in the booming industries of the central belt or to find seasonal work in the herring trade.

ERSKINE BEVERIDGE 1895 SC684175

ABOVE

A row of cottages merges into the landscape of Glen Strae by Loch Awe. Housing conditions in rural communities were generally poor, providing cramped accommodation with people living, cooking and sleeping in one room.

GEORGE WASHINGTON WILSON c1870

DP074546

The irregular timber frame of a bobbin mill sits like a ramshackle frontier house at Kinrara near Aviemore. Crafted from wood, bobbins held yarn spun from linen or wool and were important tools for weavers. Small businesses were crucial for employment and local economies throughout rural Scotland, with crafts and industries like grain milling, timber sawing and blacksmithing providing vital services to the agricultural community.

1893 DP071761

Until the development of industrial milling in the twentieth century, mills were an integral part of every rural community, town or burgh. Often water-powered, most landowners had a mill, and any grain grown on the land was taken there for grinding. In 1854, Seton Mill was just one of 34 mills recorded in rural East Lothian for grinding corn, with a further 37 for flour or barley.

WILLIAM NOTMAN COLLECTION c1890
DP075659

Modern day Braemar was originally two villages separated by the Cluny Water with Castleton on the east side and Auchendryne on the west. This mill seems to have provided a service to both communities. In 1851, according to *Black's Picturesque Tourist of Scotland*, there were "few if any new lodging-houses for health-seeking citizens; but it has two excellent inns for the tourist, where he may be positively on occasion saturated with venison and grouse".

GEORGE WASHINGTON WILSON c1880
DP073927

A rural couple is framed in an idealised scene of pastoral life in a photograph, perhaps staged for commercial purposes, in the Perthshire village of Muthill. Households often kept a number of animals to provide basic commodities such as milk, eggs or meat.

c1890 DP070830

Ploughshares lie arranged and ready for repair or sale in a blacksmiths' yard near Banff. Agriculture was dependent on sturdy iron tools and equipment and, with the horse replacing the oxen as the popular beast of burden, further trade came from shoeing the animals to allow them to travel on the hard, metalled roads.

c1893 DP074759

By the late nineteenth century, only the
skeleton of the ancient town and thriving sea
port of Culross remained. With its coalmines
flooded and its iron industry destroyed
by urban competition, an atmosphere of
dilapidation had sunk into many of its
crumbling buildings, as here at the Tron Shop.
ERSKINE BEVERIDGE c1883 SC1129147

RIGHT
One of three fishing villages on Gamrie
Bay on the Moray Firth the houses of
Gardenstown were built on ledges cut into
a steep cliff. Cobbled streets led from the
fishermen's houses down to the shore and
the harbour. In 1881, there were 98 fishing
boats based at Gardenstown.
c1893 DP074758

GIFT TO
THE TOWN OF
MOFFAT
FROM
WILLIAM COLVIN
OF CRAIGIELANDS
1875

Commemorating the town's time as a centre for wool production, the bronze 'Moffat Ram' was a gift in 1875 from William Colvin of Craigielands, Beattock, a wealthy sheepbreeder and stockman. A key stop-off for sheep and cattle drovers in the eighteenth and early nineteenth centuries, in the Victorian era Moffat became a popular spa destination for tourists. Water "strongly impregnated with sulphur and various salts" was piped to the public baths in the town, and a hydropathic hotel opened in 1878.

? GEORGE WASHINGTON WILSON c1880
DP073887

Thurso - Cooking Smithy -

In 1876 Thurso hosted an Exhibition of Art
and Industry. "I saw that Exhibition", J T Reid
commented in 1876 , "and did find it a rare treat
to see so far north some of the choice gems of
painting from South Kensington. The fruit of
the enlivening the quaint old northern town has
got through the Exhibition may be seen by-and-
bye." Photographer George Washington Wilson's
composition highlights the positioning of Thurso
within a typically agricultural setting of flagstone-

Stranraer - George St - St George Hotel -

The photographer has worked entirely with the cooperation of many of the people of Stranraer to capture the bustle and life of this market town which, according to Francis H Groome writing in the *Ordnance Gazetteer of Scotland*, consists "chiefly of modern streets and possessing a large amount of handsome or elegant architecture, presents very little regularity or tastefulness of arrangement". Both this print and the image of Thurso were purchased and annotated in a

Too large to enter the confines of the harbour, a trading ketch anchors in Crail's natural inlet. The village once hosted one of the largest medieval craft markets in Europe, with merchants arriving by ship from far afield with their many different wares. In 1852, sixteen boats were based in Crail and it was suggested that the "inconvenience of its harbour" explained why only potatoes and grain were exported, and coal imported.

ERSKINE BEVERIDGE c1890 SC388582

There were once as many as 30,000 vessels engaged in herring fishing on the east coast of Scotland and, as the nineteenth century progressed, the industry became one of the largest in Europe. By 1881, Crail had 50 fishermen and 34 boats.

ERSKINE BEVERIDGE c1890 SC388583

ABOVE

In Stonehaven, the fishing industry was the backbone of the town, with over 100 boats working from the harbour and larger ships taking cargoes of herring to the distant Baltic seaports. By 1883, from the town and neighbouring villages, there were almost 700 fishermen and boys, as well as some 400 others, employed in the trade.

c1890 SC936446

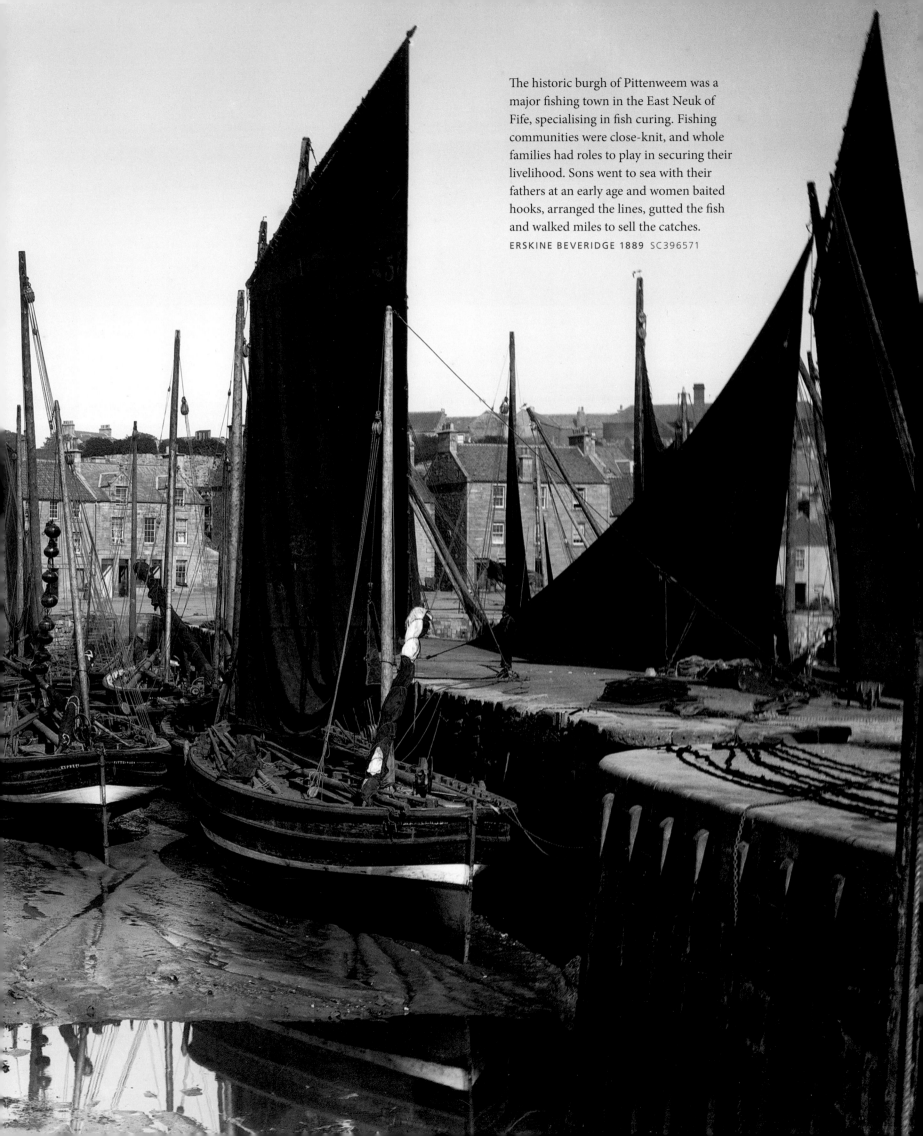

The historic burgh of Pittenweem was a major fishing town in the East Neuk of Fife, specialising in fish curing. Fishing communities were close-knit, and whole families had roles to play in securing their livelihood. Sons went to sea with their fathers at an early age and women baited hooks, arranged the lines, gutted the fish and walked miles to sell the catches.

ERSKINE BEVERIDGE 1889 SC396571

Said to be the oldest continuously occupied castle in Scotland, Dunvegan on Skye is the ancient seat of the MacLeod Chieftains of Harris and Lewis. While parts of the structure date back to the thirteenth or fourteenth century, building works undertaken hundreds of years later to 'medievalise' the castle received the approval of the great chivalric revivalist Sir Walter Scott.

c1890 SC948763

In 1887, William Arrol, the great Victorian engineer and future MP, purchased 50 acres of land at Seafield, Ayr, to build a grand Italianate mansion. In the words of his biographer Sir Robert Purvis he had decided to "prepare himself a place where in the intervals of his work he might enjoy retired leisure. The place needed to be near enough to the Dalmarnock works to enable him by railway to return and ply his daily task there. But … it was to be far enough away to free him from the smoke and noisy turmoil of that busiest of places, the great city of Glasgow".

H BEDFORD LEMERE 1890 SC695367

Light streams across the polished wooden
floor of the elegantly furnished music room
of Duntreath Castle in Stirlingshire. Dating
back to the fourteenth century, this once
imposing castle had fallen into disrepair when
Sir Archibald Edmonstone began restoration
work in 1857. In the 1890s Duntreath was
extensively remodelled by the architect Sydney
Mitchell as a Franco-Scottish palace.

H BEDFORD LEMERE 1898 SC694760

Giant ferns, exotic plants, an ornate
fountain and a fish pond surround the
walkways of the hothouse in William
Arrol's Seafield mansion in Ayr.
Conservatories were popular features in
Victorian country houses, with companies
like Mackenzie & Moncur specialising
in their often extensive manufacture and
construction.

H BEDFORD LEMERE 1890 SC695386

Built in 1870 for the wealthy silk merchant Sir James Mackenzie, the grand mansion house of Glenmuick transports the startlingly bold architecture of the Victorian industrialist to the wild vistas of Royal Deeside.

GEORGE WASHINGTON WILSON c1875 DP073924

This Victorian Life

In 1918, Giles Lytton Strachey – critic, biographer and Bloomsbury Group provocateur – wrote in the preface to his book *Eminent Victorians* of the difficulty of reanimating an era that had, up to that point, been assessed only by stiff, scholarly works that were "as familiar as the cortege of the undertaker", with the "same air of slow, funereal barbarism". "The history of the Victorian age will never be written", opined Strachey, "we know too much about it … It is not by the direct method of a scrupulous narration that the explorer of the past can hope to depict that singular epoch. If he is wise he will adopt a subtler strategy."

For Strachey this alternative approach involved shining a "sudden, revealing searchlight", into the lives of some of the nineteenth century's most virtuous paragons: Cardinal Manning, Florence Nightingale, General Gordon of Khartoum and Dr Thomas Arnold, headmaster of Rugby public school. His critical, energetic biographies – some would say character assassinations – arrived as a revelation to the cultural commentators of the early twentieth century. Strachey's audacious, mischievous treatment of near-canonised Victorian worthies – which highlighted all that was callous, pompous and absurd in his subjects – was a classic act of rebellion by a new generation against its elders. It was so influential that not only did it destroy forever the Victorian era's pretensions to moral superiority, it also pushed popular opinion on the nineteenth century to an opposite extreme – from age of progress, innovation and pre-eminence, to age of puritan, belligerent prejudice. Strachey's final, damning verdict of the Victorians as "mouthing, bungling hypocrites" very quickly became received wisdom. His intention had been to debunk myths and highlight the role of the flawed, real individual in history: "Human beings are too important to be treated as mere symptoms of the past", he wrote. "They have a value which is independent of any temporal processes – which is eternal and must be felt for its own sake." But it went even further than that. For a nation still mired in the horror of the First World War, the impulse to connect Strachey's sketches of Victorian egotism and vanity to everything that had gone wrong in the new century – including the appalling international conflict – was too strong to resist.

As one set of clichés was demolished, another rose to take its place. The word 'Victorian' became synonymous with 'hypocrisy'. White had become black, and all the shades of grey – or patterned chintz – in between, were lost. Images of stern, repressed patriarchs ruling their families on strict routine, and corseted, anxious mistresses shrouding piano legs for decency's sake, took hold. Beneath the respectable, buttoned-up exteriors were dark, unspoken desires – a society split down the middle between surface and secret lives, public monumentality and private sublimation, moral self-righteousness and clandestine sin.

Photography has played a significant role in perpetuating these stereotypes. Invented in the 1840s and refined and popularised in subsequent decades, a whole society – quite understandably – went crazy for this most potent of recording

ABOVE

Standing on a chair in Kinnaird House
in Perthshire, young Henry Forrester is
kilted and posed like a miniature adult.
In nineteenth century photographic
portraiture, children were often pictured
in fancy dress to appeal to parental whims.
As ever, Queen Victoria had set the trend,
dressing her sons and daughters as drummer
boys and shepherdesses in mass-produced
royal portraits.

c1890 DP045073

RIGHT

Like Alice in her Wonderland, a young
girl sits lost in thought in a photograph
labelled 'Grotto, Blairgowrie House'. An
age that had begun by seeing children
as essential to the industrial work-
place – small hands and bodies best for
mending machinery – ended with a cult
of childhood innocence, celebrated and
sentimentalised in literature, print, paintings and photography.

1886 DP074530

A family lines up for their picture beside a well-dressed man in a horse and trap. Throughout the 1880s, the costs of cameras and glass plates fell considerably, allowing more and more people to record moments from their everyday lives.
1890 SC790941

Along the river Jed, boys have been arranged carefully to contribute to the sentimental composition of this photograph of Jedburgh Abbey.
J HAY c1887 SC1139054

Elena Cecilia Anne Kinloch – daughter of Sir George Kinloch – celebrates her marriage to George Palmer, a civil engineer, at Meigle House in Perthshire.
1886 SC890093

Margaret and Andrew Anderson MD, of 2 Woodside Crescent, Glasgow, are captured here in two typically formal portraits. Many early photographs were considered forbidding and disagreeable, and one of the skills of the Victorian practitioner was to position his subjects in such a way that the final image would be acceptable. There was a great deal of deliberate artifice in these pictures as people were paying for – and expected – flattering and atmospheric likenesses. Women were often arranged in thoughtful repose – leaning on a table, with the prop of an open book, as here – while for men, presenting an aura of dignified authority was crucial.

c1880 SC892293

ABOVE
Taken at Lennoxlove House in East Lothian, a woman sits working at a treadle sewing machine. **1887–1900** DP074341

RIGHT
Patented by the French photographer André Disdéri in 1854, the *carte de visite* portrait involved a multi-lensed camera taking a number of small images which were cut up and placed on individual card mounts. Between 1861 and 1867 it has been estimated that over 300 million *cartes* were produced each year, with likenesses of famous people purchased as enthusiastically as personal portraits. These portraits come from an album which includes Dunbeath Castle in Caithness.

1861–78 DP028980 & DP028981

ABOVE AND RIGHT

While servants line up nervously for a
photograph at St Fort in Fife, the pipe-
clasping masters and guests of the house,
dressed in tweeds and spats, confidently
eye the camera. Intriguingly the image
of the men is captioned 'A Group of the
Unemployed' – perhaps as a teasing reference to their privileged lives of sport and
leisure. **1895** SC864350 & DP007390

Sir Walter Scott's early nineteenth century novels – with their sentimentalised depictions of chivalry and medievalism – had made the writer a cult figure in Victorian society. His visions of benevolent castle communities as models for social harmony captivated aristocratic landowners and fuelled the passion for all things baronial. Many Scottish nobles looked to recreate Scott's misty-eyed environments, taking their cues from the Highland informality of Queen Victoria's Balmoral to run households based on the principle of ethical equality between master and servant.

CLOCKWISE FROM TOP LEFT

Gamekeepers cottage, St Fort, Fife
1894 SC939865

Methven Castle, Perthshire
1860–70 DP073558

Stableboy and 'Hornbeam', St Fort, Fife
1893–96 DP073558

Grass-cutter, Wemyss Castle, Fife
1870 DP073840

Innocence and the eternal – here the
photographer frames children playing in
the graveyard of the ruined Kirkton Church
at Burntisland in Fife.
J HAY 1880 SC1106547

Known as 'Aunt Henry', Jemima Watt was the matriarch of the Beveridge family, a well-known Dunfermline dynasty. Her nephew, Erskine Beveridge, captures her here at the grand age of 88, two years before her death, and 40 years beyond average adult life expectancy at the end of the Victorian era.

ERSKINE BEVERIDGE c1883 SC1129266

ABOVE
Members of the congregation of Lismore Parish Church – part of the medieval Cathedral of Argyll and once the location of a sixth century monastery – gather in a sparse, overgrown graveyard. While urban living challenged ideas of belief, in rural communities religion remained a binding, pervasive influence. As photographers looked beyond portraiture – with its obvious initial novelty – they began to record seemingly less staged scenes of everyday life.

ERSKINE BEVERIDGE 1882 SC500617

Looking out from the communion table towards the empty gallery, the architectural photographer Harry Bedford Lemere captures the solemn grace of St Cuthbert's Parish Church in Edinburgh. Designed in a renaissance style by architect Hippolyte Jean Blanc and completed in 1895, St Cuthbert's was built on the site of an ancient church dating back to the twelfth century. Amidst the spiritual chaos of the city, new churches rose as architectural beacons for the many looking to reinforce or reaffirm their faith.

H BEDFORD LEMERE 1895 SC717186

Between the towering medieval grandeur of Glasgow Cathedral and the distant chimney stacks of the industrial city, mausoleums, crypts, obelisks and headstones rise up to form the Necropolis, a monumental Victorian tribute to the dead. Inspired by the celebrated Père Lachaise cemetery in Paris, the graveyard was the dream of Dr John Strang, Chamberlain in the Merchants House. For Strang, "A garden cemetery is the sworn foe to preternatural fear and superstition … Adorn the sepulchre, and the frightful visions which visit the midnight pillow will disappear … A garden cemetery and monumental decoration afford the most convincing tokens of a nation's progress in civilization and in the arts which are its result."

GEORGE WASHINGTON WILSON pre1877
DP073879

FORTH BRIDGE WORKS
INTERIOR OF GIRDER
10 JULY. 85. N°

Iron and Steam

"On the still morning air, the heavy rumble of the trains can be heard from afar, and in the grey light of dawn, travellers by the west coast train can see across the lagoon of Montrose basin the lighted carriages of the rival train. Now fractions of minutes determine the result. Excitement is at fever heat, a tension which is not released among the passengers until the tail lights of the winner are seen whirled past the signal box."

This was how the *Dundee Advertiser* reported the great railway race of the summer of 1895. Throughout the months of June, July and August the Caledonian and North British Railway Companies competed with public insouciance, yet private fury, to travel from London to Aberdeen in the fastest time. With each passing day, minutes and hours were knocked off the journey until, on the early morning of 23 August, a Caledonian west coast train arrived in Aberdeen eight hours and 32 minutes after leaving London – eight clear minutes faster than the quickest North British east coast service. Amid claims of victory – and counter-claims of short-carriage trains, corrupt signalmen and even the absence of any race at all – the quest for speed was declared over.

If identifying a clear victor between the two great companies was arguable, the history leading up to the contest was littered with rather more obvious winners and losers. For over 60 years a fierce and often dirty war had been fought for control of the Scottish railroads: a war that had seen the two companies deceive their shareholders and descend into toxic debt; that had sliced up farmlands and carelessly smashed through towns and cities; and that, most remarkably, had produced the longest and the largest railway bridges the world had ever seen.

Every war needs it heroes and its martyrs. In the Victorian era, the engineer was the peacetime equivalent of the victorious soldier. He could be a superstar, a 'boys-own' embodiment of brave ingenuity, building the modern world with his bare hands. It was a heady image and one that captured the fancy of both public and practitioners. As the nineteenth century's constructors and innovators pioneered new techniques, they also sought greater challenges, intoxicated by notions of celebrity and addicted to the opium of grandeur.

It was the North British Railway Company's desperation to cross the Forth and Tay estuaries, and break the Caledonian stranglehold over the route to Aberdeen, that gave a man called Thomas Bouch the opportunity to enter the pantheon of legendary engineers. Bouch, perhaps a little more by luck than by reputation, found himself designing simultaneously a two-mile long, continuous girder bridge, and a gigantic, eight-columned, 600ft tall double suspension bridge. In scale and boldness, the plans had no parallel anywhere else on earth. With the incredible stretch of the Tay Bridge completed in 1878, Bouch turned his full attention to the Forth – the last link for an unbroken east coast line and the masterpiece that would confirm his reputation as the world's greatest bridge builder.

But the idealised engineer stands or falls by his creations. On the night of 28 December 1879, in the midst of a fierce storm, the 4.30pm train from Edinburgh crashed from the collapsed central spans of Bouch's Tay Bridge into the icy waters below. While true fault remains the subject of conjecture, what mattered most was that the disaster had shaken a cherished Victorian certainty – that of the infallibility of the era's technological marvels. The hero had turned villain.

The response was swift, robust and unsentimental. Bouch was out. A new, hulking, double-track Tay Bridge was designed by William Henry Barlow. The Forth crossing was re-imagined by Benjamin Baker as a series of colossal steel cantilevers. And William Arrol, the working class son of a Renfrewshire cotton spinner, would build them both.

The architecture of the two bridges became an exercise in psychological reassurance. The Forth Bridge in particular was an iconic statement of Victorian fortitude, its construction works awe-inspiring in their scale. Six enormous caissons were floated out into the estuary and then sunk to the seabed. Men climbed 89ft below the water to excavate earth from cramped pressurised chambers to allow the tower foundations to lie at the right level. At the other extreme, rivet gangs swarmed 340ft above the Forth, heating their rivets in portable furnaces before fitting them to the emerging superstructure's dizzying network of steel girders.

Long before its completion, the bridge was a tourist attraction, a futuristic monument that inspired amazement and terror in almost equal measures. A sense of technological horror was evident in William Morris' lecture to the Art Congress of 1889. "Every improvement in the art of engineering made the use of iron more ugly, until at last they had that supreme specimen of ugliness, the Forth Bridge." Alfred Waterhouse, one of the era's leading architects demurred, "One feature especially delights me – the absence of ornament. Any architectural detail borrowed from any style would have been out of place in such a work. As it is the bridge is a style unto itself."

Baker, in the self-mythologising rhetoric typical of the visionary nineteenth century engineer, described his creation as "a romantic chapter from a fairytale of science". The Forth Bridge, the steel giant of this most Victorian of fairytales, had crossed a boundary to a modern age. In a century of great engineering adventures, it was unrivalled as the greatest.

PREVIOUS PAGES
A man stands framed by the colossal steel symmetry of the 42nd girder of the Forth Rail Bridge. "The Engineers with their gigantic works sweep everything before them in this Victoria era", wrote the Bridge's designer Benjamin Baker.
? EVELYN CAREY 1885 DP010187

RIGHT
Workers pause to have their photograph taken during the construction of a 'skewback'. These multi-strut joints were the meeting points for the webs of steel tubing that formed the superstructure of the enormous Forth Bridge cantilevers. Much of the Bridge was first assembled – as here – at an immense workshop at Queensferry, where the steel could be manipulated and the designs tested. As *The Scotsman* reported, "The whole of the bridge is built in large sections in the works at Queensferry and rivet fixtures tried so that no difficulty may be experienced in fitting up when the material is sent out to the piers … It thus comes about that the whole of the bridge will have been built twice ere it is finally erected."
? EVELYN CAREY 1885 DP010202

In this stark photograph, so exposed with light that it resembles a line drawing, it almost appears as if the draughting engineer has still to complete his work by sketching in a final central span. Instead, what this image captures is the chilling simplicity of the Tay Bridge disaster of December 1879, a tragedy which claimed the lives of 72 people travelling from Edinburgh to Dundee. The thin line of the longest bridge in the world has been completely erased by the winter storms, leaving behind only the dark stumps of its supporting piers.

VALENTINES OF DUNDEE 1879 DP073894

At the end of the kaleidoscopic, jagged metal tunnel of a giant Forth Bridge tube, the faint figures of a group of workmen gaze out from a shadowy chamber. Each piece of studded, riveted steel used to make up the 3.5m diameter tube was individually labelled to ease the process of disassembly and reconstruction. Rejecting cast and wrought iron as building materials, the designers of the mammoth Forth crossing had resolved instead to create the world's first-ever steel bridge, using over 54,000 tons of the metal in the final structure. As William Westhofen, a mechanical engineer from Mainz and the biographer of the bridge project, wrote, "a more uniform, a more homogenous, a more satisfactory material could not be wished for".

? EVELYN CAREY 1885 DP010191

FORTH BRIDGE WORKS
INTERIOR OF 12 FOOT TUBE
9 JULY. 85.   Nº 39.

400 tons in weight and 70ft in diameter, the giant, metal cylinders known as caissons were constructed at South Queensferry and floated out into the Forth to form the foundations for Benjamin Baker's ambitious superstructure design. Once they had been manoeuvered into position, the hollow structures were filled with concrete and sunk to the seabed. A space was left void as an excavation chamber at the foot of the caisson, and shafts were cast through the concrete to allow diggers access to it so they could remove earth and allow the foundations to settle at the right depth.

? EVELYN CAREY 1885 DP010248, DP010251 & DP010218

Caisson workers found themselves in an electrically lit, 70ft wide and 7ft high chamber compressed between thousands of tons of concrete and the seabed. Water was prevented from entering by compressed air which, when it regularly escaped out into the sea, filled the chamber with a fine mist. Diggers laboured under the constant fear that the weight of concrete above their heads might force the caisson down into the clay and crush them. Yet, as *The Illustrated London News* reported in 1889, "So perfectly was everything arranged in these caissons that even visitors were allowed to descend and inspect them." The paper continued to marvel at this peculiar environment deep below the Forth. "One day a number of salmon forced their way under the caisson … It was supposed that these fish … by chance had come upon the movement produced by the air escaping which is constantly being pumped into the caissons, had headed against it and thus found their way as strange but not unwelcome visitors into one of the sights of the Forth Bridge."

? EVELYN CAREY 1885 DP010261

FORTH BRIDGE WORKS
MOORING BLOCK 30 TON
19 MAY. 85.

FORTH BRIDGE WORKS
Nº 4 CAISSON
9 JULY, 85. Nº 37.

While 'briggers' stand to attention on a 30-ton mooring block, a worker looks down from the scaffold of an air compression engine. An elaborate contraption of valves, gauges, pipes, pistons and wheels, the engine was vital to the process of securing the Forth Bridge foundations to the riverbed. Positioned by the entrances to caissons, they created airlocks allowing diggers to enter airshafts and descend to excavation chambers up to 89ft below high water level.

In his biography of the bridge project, William Westhofen described the incident that left the number four caisson tilting precariously on the seabed. "On New Year's Day, 1885, an exceptionally high tide occurred, followed by an equally exceptional low ebb, and the caisson sank deeply into the mud … Not being built high enough, the water soon flowed in and filled it completely." The accident was thought to have occurred as a result of an unsupervised foreman forgetting to leave open a valve that would have allowed the seawater to escape. Work to right the caisson – pictured here in July 1885 – was not complete until October of that same year.

In his memoir of William Arrol, Sir Robert Purvis described the near-dreamlike emergence of the Forth Bridge. "From year to year the wonder grew, as the mighty piers slowly rose out of the sea, and the ascending columns climbed ever higher and higher." With the cantilevers sitting on the water like three massive, skeletal galleons, in March 1888 *The Scotsman* reported the remarkable process of bridging the gaps as the existing superstructures acted as their own scaffolding. "The workers today are practically standing on their labours of yesterday. As soon as a fresh round of steel plates is added to the tubes, or an additional girder section riveted to the top arms, the platforms with their freight of men and cranes and other mechanical appliances are slid out correspondingly and a new piece of work is begun … Every piece of work done becomes the basis for another advance, and the Forth Bridge men labour much in the same way as the Esquimaux who ascends the ice cliff by cutting steps, one after another in its face."

ALEXANDER INGLIS 1887 SC361741

In the shadow of Calton Jail and the Burial Ground, coal wagons rest in the sidings of the goods yard at the eastern entrance to Edinburgh's Waverley Station. The North British Railway Company had completely underestimated the effect the opening of the Forth Bridge would have on its anti-quated Waverley terminus. With increased traffic leading to severe delays, an editorial in *The Times* in August 1890 pointed out that a blockage of even half an hour at Waverley, "will be felt in the derangement of the service 10 to 15 hours afterwards as far west as Plymouth and as far north as Wick".

ALEXANDER INGLIS 1892–1901 SC1120460

In 1892 the total reconstruction of Waverley Station began, the works sprawling across an enormous site that extended several storeys up from the depths of the glacial valley to the level of the North Bridge and Princes Street. On completion, Waverley provided the largest railway accommodation in Britain after London's Waterloo Station. ? ALEXANDER INGLIS 1890s
SC370939 & SC1092519

As well as providing an inspirational canvas for the Victorian era's often narcissistic superstar engineers, the railways also had a huge impact on the development of many industries first established in the eighteenth and early nineteenth centuries. In this photograph, the three steepling chimneys of James and John Clark's huge 'Atlantic' and 'Pacific' cotton thread mills rise up from behind the old Paisley bridge to dominate the town skyline. Although the mills were first established in 1802, it was the large-scale manufacture and distribution of sewing machines that acted as the catalyst for a huge boom in the cotton trade. The Atlantic Mill was built in 1873 for cotton spinning, and the Pacific Mill was added in 1878 for doubling, the process of making thread from yarn.

c1878 SC897016

Staff line up outside the Roslin Gunpowder Mills around 1860. Founded by Messrs Hay and Merricks, the Mills first began production in Roslin Glen around 1804. The water power of the River Esk and the proximity to the Forth made Roslin an ideal site for industrial activity – the famous carpet manufacturer Richard Whytock also opened a factory in the area in 1868. The constant risk of explosion meant that workers were required to wear special woollen clothing – jackets and trousers had bone buttons, no metal of any kind was allowed, and there were no pockets. Upon arrival at work both men and women were searched for any matches or objects which could make a spark or cause an explosion.

c1860 DP070953

A great slate archway formed the symbolic entrance to the East Laroch quarry at Ballachulish on the south shore of the sea arm of Loch Leven. First quarried on a small scale at Laroch farm in 1693, by the late nineteenth century slate had become a huge industry in Ballachulish, with the works supplying most of the slate for western Scotland, and exporting to England and America.

GEORGE WASHINGTON WILSON c1870

DP074547

Iron, steam and slate – workers stand by the boiler of a steam-driven crane at the Ballachulish quarry. The quarries employed over 400 men on a quarry face 1,400m long, with the finished supplies of slate transported through Loch Linnhe to the sea.

c1900 SC1075448

Found in an album of Northern Lighthouse Board photographs, a peculiar cast of characters pose for the camera on Ailsa Craig's gas-powered north foghorn. Constructed between 1883 and 1886, the foghorn was one of two built to support Thomas and David Stevenson's oil-burning lighthouse.

pre1901 DP049359

Visit Scotland

In the late eighteenth century, James Macpherson, a young Highland schoolmaster, claimed to have discovered and compiled precious pieces of a great, lost, story of Scotland. *Fragments of Ancient Poetry Collected in the Highlands of Scotland,* and *Fingal, an Ancient Epic Poem*, were, he said, verse translations of an original, third century masterwork – the epic tales of the blind poet Ossian, who had sung of the heroic struggles of the legendary warrior Finn. Although the authenticity of Macpherson's remarkable finds were soon questioned – most notably by the foremost man of English letters Dr Samuel Johnson – the sceptics were too late. The controversial works were already on their way to creating a European-wide, cultural phenomenon. As the nineteenth century poet and critic Matthew Arnold wrote, "All Europe felt the power of Ossian's Celtic melancholy."

Through the mouthpiece of Macpherson, a bard of the early dark ages enraptured a continent. For Voltaire, the achingly romantic saga of a noble Celtic race bore direct comparison with the *Iliad* and the *Odyssey*, and made Ossian a "Scottish Homer". Schiller, Schubert and Brahms were admirers along with Goethe, the foremost poet of the age and the author of *Faust,* who incorporated Ossian and his meditations on love and isolation into his first novel, *The Sorrows of Young Werther.* Napoleon became an avid fan after first reading the works in Italian translation and would often carry copies into battle. "I like Ossian", the emperor said, "for the same reason that I like to hear the whisper of the wind and the waves of the sea". To decorate his salons and palaces, he commissioned some of the greatest French painters of the era to capture Ossian on canvas. Anne Louise Girodet's *Ossian Receiving the Ghosts of French Heroes* took pride of place in the Chateau de Malmaison, while *The Dream of Ossian* by Jean-Auguste-Dominique Ingres was produced to adorn Napoleon's bedroom ceiling in Rome's Quirinal Palace, his residence during the French occupation of the Italian capital.

Ossian had conquered cultural Europe. And, at the same time, Macpherson – whether a vessel for ancient verse or an opportunistic fraud – had reinvented Scotland and its landscapes in the popular imagination. Barren wildernesses emerged reborn from mythological mists. Highland heaths once considered gloomy were rediscovered as the sublime settings that had long ago witnessed the dramas of a nation's soulful ancestors. In Ossian, the Romantic Movement sweeping Europe had found an irresistible muse and figurehead, and – much more tangible than that – a place of pilgrimage. Scotland had emerged as a potent brand. Inadvertently, Macpherson had pulled off a spectacularly successful marketing coup. Just as the concept of travel as an end in itself – rather than to reach a destination – was coalescing into the new industry of tourism, Ossian had imbedded one thought in the collective consciousness of Europe: visit Scotland.

The Celtic bard had grown beyond Macpherson and become a merchandising sensation. He was celebrated in operas, plays, pantomimes and exhibitions. Even the composer Felix Mendelssohn got in on the act, writing his *Hebrides Overture* in

1829 after a visit to the Isle of Staffa – the reputed home of 'Fingal's Cave'. As Ossian's poems were largely vague on locations, anywhere that could claim even the remotest connection to the legend – "the brown heath that Ossian was want to tread" as the novelist Tobias Smollett put it – was suffused with a stirring atmosphere of love and loss.

With the very landscape growing into a precious commodity, it was not long before the first appearance of what would go on to become the travellers' bible – the guidebook. In the 1760s, there were just seven books describing travel tours of Scotland. By the 1820s there were 53. In 1832, over a six month period, the fashion-able *Court Magazine* included feature pieces on notable aspects of Scottish tourist life in each of its six issues, including, 'A Pleasure Party in the Highlands', 'The Widow's Summer Evening: A Scotch Ballad' and 'Deer Stalking' – a special offer, for an extra two shillings and sixpence, offered 'Landscape Illustrations of the Prose and Poetical Works of Sir Walter Scott'. Most notable of all, though, was a guide released in 1846, entitled a *Hand Book of a Trip to Scotland*. Its author was a temperance campaigner from Market Harborough in Leicestershire – and his name was Thomas Cook.

Cook's brochure offered an 800-mile round-trip of the land of Ossian, Scott and Burns – and all for the price of just one guinea. Although the trip experienced a number of logistical mishaps, the 500 paid-up members of the world's first package tour were received in Scotland with near unbridled enthusiasm: Glasgow greeted the excursionists with a gun salute and a pipe band, Edinburgh met the party with more bands again, and a special musical evening was organised to welcome what Cook called "English pleasure money … to the heart of the Highlands". For Cook, travel was a classless pleasure with money the only determinant of access. In reality this at first tended towards wealthy professionals – doctors, lawyers, clergymen and their wives and children – yet that did not stop certain sectors of society reacting with repulsion to the prospect of mass tourism. The *Pall Mall Gazette* mocked the tourists' "ignorance, stupidity and incapacity for enjoyment", while Cook himself was pre-sented with the suggestion that "places of interest should be excluded from the gaze of the common people, and … kept only for the interest of the 'select' of society". His response was plain and unwavering: "It is too late in this day of progress to talk such exclusive nonsense; God's earth, with all its fullness and beauty, is for the people; and railroads and steamboats are the result of the common light of science, and are for the people also."

This was a new kind of industrial revolution – a revolution of leisure and free time; a revolution in the common understanding of history, culture, landscapes and their material worth. The Victorians loved nothing better than a show, and tourism called 'roll up, roll up' to the world at large. For a small fee, the whole of Scotland had become a stage.

PREVIOUS PAGES
Beyond the baronial elegance of the Loch Awe Hotel awaits the romantic Scotland of literature and myth. Built on a rocky loch-side outcrop, the hotel opened in 1881 and was situated almost immediately above a railway station and a steamer pier.
GEORGE WASHINGTON WILSON c1890
SC715064

RIGHT
The expanding tourist industry in Scotland coincided with the development of photo-graphy, with albums often created as mementos. G M Simpson from Southern Queensland in Australia compiled these montages of Scottish scenery around 1880, after a family tour of Europe and the United States. The majority of the images are likely to be from the firm of George Washington Wilson in Aberdeen, together with James Valentine in Dundee, pioneers in the manufacture of photographs for the mass market. These annotated pages from the album show two popular areas on the tourist trail: the Scottish Borders with Tibbie Shiels Inn, St Mary's Loch, the Eildon Hills and Abbotsford; and Stirling with the Castle, the newly built Wallace Monument and Stirling Bridge.
? GEORGE WASHINGTON WILSON pre1880
DP077213 & DP077323

Tibbie Shiels Inn. head of St Mary's Loch.

Eildon Hills near Melrose. River Tweed and Bemerside House. looking east. Melrose some miles to right.

St Mary's Loch. looking West.

Abbotsford and Tweed River.

View from Stirling Castle. shewing windings of Forth. old bridge. Wallace Monument.

Stirling Castle from Back Walk.

Stirling Castle from Cathedral. Virgin Martyrs Memorial.

Stirling Bridge.

Sir Walter Scott was influential throughout Europe in establishing Scotland as a tourist destination. Writing in 1863, Cuthbert Bede described Scott's Borders home at Abbotsford as, "the Mecca of the Scotch tourists, and during the summer months the stream of pilgrims is incessantly flowing towards Scott's shrine". The original Abbotsford farm was taken over by Scott in 1811 and extended into a mansion, with sculptured stones from ruined castles and abbeys across Scotland built into its walls.
1860–70 DP074544

With an expanding network of transportation, the tourist could visit attractions in many of the more northern parts of Scotland. Published in 1871, *A Guide to the Ruins of Elgin Cathedral* promised that a visit to the thirteenth century site would "reward the travel of many miles, for the more minutely it is examined the more will the traveller be surprised at the profusion of varied sculpture everywhere to be seen in the ruins around him".
c1900 SC1161649

ABOVE

"We entered a most magnificent decorated barge, drawn by three horses, ridden by postillions in scarlet … the view of the hills were very fine indeed; but the eleven locks we had to go through were tedious." So Queen Victoria described her voyage on the Crinan Canal in 1847. Built between 1793 and 1801, the Canal connects Ardrishaig on Loch Gilp with Crinan – pictured here.

VALENTINES OF DUNDEE pre1888 SC753469

TOP RIGHT

Designed by the Glasgow architect James Miller for the Glasgow & South Western Railway Company, the impressive Princes Pier Railway Station in Greenock opened in 1893. Greenock had long been a popular stop for tourists taking paddle steamers to the Firth of Clyde seaside resorts of Helensburgh, Dunoon and Rothesay. Queen Victoria described the bustling scene in 1847: "At half-past twelve we reached Greenock, the port of Glasgow.

The shore and the ships were crowded with people, there being no less than thirty-nine steamers, overfilled with people, which almost all followed us! Such a thing never was seen."

H BEDFORD LEMERE 1894 SC716998

BOTTOM RIGHT

Gourock Pier Railway Station was also an embarkation point for tourists taking the steamers down the Clyde. Built for the Caledonian Railway Company in 1889, the platform's slim iron columns and arched girders supported a glass roof, with Victorian gas lamps hanging at intervals from the metalwork. A sign – enigmatically cropped here by the photographer – directed passengers, 'To The Steamers'.

H BEDFORD LEMERE 1890 SC730401

The staff of Stanley Junction Station in Perthshire stand in readiness for the next wave of passengers. With hat badges bearing the initials 'CR', the porters, engineers, signalmen, ticket office clerks and stationmaster were all employees of the great Caledonian Railway Company. The fierce rival of the North British Railway Company, the Caledonian had taken up the motto of Scotland "Nemo me impune lacessit", meaning "nobody harms me with impunity" or – as traditionally translated into Scots – "Wha daur meddle wi' me?" Its bullish intention, as outlined in the minutes of an 1845 Board meeting, was to become the national Scottish Trunk Railway and bring "the whole of Scotland" into "the Caledonian system".

c1889 DP070848

The Stanley Junction team pose for a group photograph. The station was on the line from Perth to Inverness and was also a starting point for the Strathmore line to Arbroath and further to Aberdeen. The Caledonian Railway took over the route in 1866. In the pioneering age of railway expansion, companies controlled more than just tracks and engines – their goal was to create a transport nexus for people and goods that involved owning or part-owning everything from docks, harbours and canals, to steamers and hotels.

c1889 DP070846

Described as a 'Highland Camelot', the Trossachs Hotel by Loch Achray was a popular stop for travellers making their way to Loch Katrine, the scene of Walter Scott's famous poem *The Lady of the Lake*. Visiting the hotel in 1863, Cuthbert Bede was astonished by the sheer weight of tourist traffic: "Coaches continued to arrive with full loads, apparently at half-hour intervals; and those who had come expecting to sleep at the Trossachs Hotel had to be forwarded on to Stronachlachar and Inversnaid, or to Callander."

WILLIAM NOTMAN COLLECTION c1890
SC1169322

An advertisement from 1890 described Edzell as a "beautiful village … at the foot of the Grampians, near the North Esk. Recommended by leading Physicians for healthiness and bracing air". Edzell was not connected to the railway until 1895, the same year as the opening of the Panmure Arms Hotel, pictured here.

c1900 SC1161650

"Resulting from the completion of the Callander and Oban line, a splendid new hotel has been reared by the side of Loch Awe", commented an 1881 travel article, "which to tourist and anglers will form a most attractive place of resort". The railway had opened up the remote reaches of Scotland to tourist industry investment and development. Here at Loch Awe, the transfer from train and steamer stop to luxury accommodation was made as short as possible.

WILLIAM NOTMAN COLLECTION c1890
DP076023

ABOVE

Long known for its sulphurous wells – believed to
have healing powers – in the Victorian era Moffat
grew into a popular spa town with a specially
built bath house. On the High Street, next to a
grocers shop, stands the Star Hotel, one of many
luxury residences that catered for spa visitors. Five
storeys high but only 20ft wide and 162ft long, it
is famous today as the world's narrowest hotel.

WILLIAM NOTMAN COLLECTION c1890 SC1169304

ABOVE

Hydropathy or water treatment became fashionable in Scotland in the 1850s, both as a form of treatment for illness but also for prevention. The Peebles Hydropathic, designed by John Starforth, opened in 1881, and advertisements from that same year claimed of the hotel that, "the Climate and Scenery are unsurpassed, the House comforts and arrangements most complete, and ample provision has been made for the recreation and enjoyment of visitors". Guests were offered "the energetic application of hydrotherapeutic measures" including volcanic mud baths and douches, with electrical treatments, massage and special diets also recommended. The range of outdoor activities on offer included tennis, croquet, salmon fishing on the River Tweed, shooting, and even an oval cycle track, which guests could ride on with rented bicycles.

H BEDFORD LEMERE 1894 SC683118

OPPOSITE

The Peebles Hydropathic offered a range of luxury environments for rest and recuperation. The 34m-long conservatory was described in an early hotel brochure as an "arbour of peace" with the "rarest plants", and guests were recommended to walk its length as an indoor activity in wet weather. With views over the River Tweed towards the Manor Hills, the drawing room offered a place where visitors could play cards, read and relax. And in the Hydropathic's elegant dining room – lit by the new technology of electric light – guests would dine listening to the music of the hotel's orchestra. The family group posing for their portrait in the conservatory may well be the hotel manager, Albert Max Thiem, his wife, and three of their children, who all assisted in the running of the hotel.

H BEDFORD LEMERE 1894

CLOCKWISE FROM TOP LEFT SC683109, SC683110, SC683117 & SC683111

"Everything here is romantic beyond imagination", declared an Ossian-inspired character on a Highland journey in Tobias Smollett's 1771 novel *The Expedition of Humphry Clinker*. Perception, history and literature made the landscape of Scotland all things for all people. Where for some, the Kings House Hotel – built in the seventeenth century and one of Scotland's oldest licensed inns – represented what the 1894 guidebook *By Mountain, Moor and Loch* described as a "very pleasant discovery in this forsaken waste", for others it was just a staging point to explore the spare, lonely and sublime trails of the Pass of Glencoe.

GEORGE WASHINGTON WILSON pre1877
DP073929

LEFT AND CENTRE

Founded in AD 563 by Columba, the monastery on Iona became one of the most sacred places of pilgrimage in Western Europe, a shrine to commune with the forefathers of early Christianity. Before the availability of hotel accommodation few visitors stayed more than a handful of hours, taking day trips from Oban by steamer. Here tourists pose by the fifteenth-century Maclean's Cross and the seventh century St Martin's Cross – described by Chauncy Townsend in 1840 as "some old richly-carved crosses … irresistibly tempting to a sketcher".

1850–72 DP074545

RIGHT

Atmospherically framed against a rugged mountain backdrop, the Glencoe memorial takes the form of a Celtic cross carved to resemble a tree trunk. Erected in 1883 by Mrs Ellen Burns MacDonald of Glencoe in honour of her ancestors, it commemorates the Massacre of Glencoe in 1692. History was a key attraction to the emerging tourist market and in 1894 the guidebook *By Mountain, Moor and Loch* singled out the area as a highlight: "few names appeal more vividly to the imagination than that of Glencoe … the fascination of the name is greatly due to the historical associations that linger round the place, but only

partly so, for the scenery of the Glen is universally admitted to be amongst the most impressive in these grand and solemn Western Highlands". Once again context and romanticism recast the Victorian understanding of the Scottish landscape.

LADY HENRIETTA GILMOUR 1899

SC799214

The Twa Brigs—o—Ayr — looking up —

Tam O' Shanter Inn — Ayr

Burns Birth Place - Alloway -

While smoke gouts from a lone chimney, Portobello beach is a boisterous blur of pleasure seekers. Along with the expansion of the railways and steamer services, increased leisure time for workers created a new phenomenon in tourism: the day-tripper. Seaside resorts saw streams of visitors in the summer months, and attractions and facilities sprang up to meet the demand. From donkey rides and fish and chip shops, to bathing machines, promenades and Punch and Judy, a Victorian 'day at the seaside' became a culturally iconic experience. The popularity of Portobello was such that, in 1870, a 381m-long promenade pier was constructed – complete with a pavilion and bandstand – the only one of its kind in Scotland.

c1880 DP073557

Queen Victoria first visited the old Castle at Balmoral in Aberdeenshire in 1848. Finding the area "so calm, and so solitary, all seemed to breathe freedom and peace, and to make one forget the world and its sad turmoils", she chose it as her Scottish home. Five years later the foundation stone for the new Castle was laid. Designed in the Scots Baronial style by William Smith of Aberdeen – with the assistance of Prince Albert – the Castle, with its distinctive clock tower, became a conspicuous landmark in Deeside. The Royal family moved to Balmoral in 1855, and in her diary Victoria wrote "the house is charming; the rooms delightful; the furniture, papers, everything perfection". This explicit Royal patronage brought great exposure to Scotland and its land-scapes, further enhancing the nation's nineteenth century reputation as a premier tourist escape.

GEORGE WASHINGTON WILSON pre1880
DP073925

GLASGOW CORPORATION WATER WORKS

DESIGNED IN 1855 AND 1856   ROBERT STEWART LORD PROVOST
ACT OF PARLIAMENT 1855   ANDREW ORR LORD PROVOST
WORKS COMMENCED 1856
WORKS COMPLETED 1859   ANDREW GALBRAITH LORD PROVOST
OPENED BY HER MAJESTY QUEEN VICTORIA 14 OCTOBER 1859
JOHN FREDERIC BATEMAN, ENGINEER

Do It Better

As the *Rob Roy* steamer emerged from a thick Highland smirr to arrive at the head of Loch Katrine, a crowd of some one thousand well wishers led by the Lord Provost of Glasgow prepared themselves to receive the vessel's distinguished guests. On board, an enthusiastic Prince Albert and a dutiful, but rather more reluctant, Queen Victoria looked out from the shelter of their glass viewing pavilion at the thronged welcome. Braving the sodden loch-side, the royal party made their way to the mouth of a newly constructed aqueduct tunnel to perform their ceremonial roles. As quickly as the speeches would allow, Her Majesty stepped up to pull the handle that opened one of three sluice gates, before hurrying to the warmth of the Royal Cottage, and the substantial roast lunch that waited inside.

At almost that same moment, bells rang out from the church towers of Glasgow, and cannon burst from the ramparts of Stirling Castle. 14 October 1859 was un-accountably a day for great celebration. While fine wine topped up royal glasses, cascading through a network of 34 miles of aqueducts, tunnels and pipes was Glasgow's first 50 million gallons of fresh Highland water. The Loch Katrine works had taken four years to construct, had spent five more in development and planning limbo, and had cost over £700,000. Yet Glasgow's civic leaders had undoubtedly overseen a remarkable triumph. No longer would the city's water supply be drawn from the diseased slough of the Clyde. Instead it could rely on the soft water of the Trossachs, the pure source immortalised by Walter Scott in *The Lady of the Lake*.

The Water Commission hailed this as "one of the largest and most comprehensive schemes for the supply of water which has yet been accomplished". A city that had previously drunk and bathed from vile, insanitary wells – with water often described as having the colour of sherry – had, by good economy, brought fresh supplies from a rural reservoir to serve the needs of its people. In the typically parsimonious words of the *Glasgow Daily Herald*, this was "a fact most highly appreciated by a community thirsty for good water on the one hand and abhorrent of high taxing rates on the other".

The opening of the Loch Katrine works was more than just another marvel of Victorian engineering. It also marked a shift in the balance of the beliefs that governed urban life. Emboldened by this success, from the late 1860s Glasgow embarked upon a series of reforms which moved the dynamic of the city away from unre-strained commerce, and began to link civic identity with popularly elected municipal authorities. Cities were becoming known not just by the activities of their industry, but also by the rhetoric and reforms of their councils.

In this respect, Glasgow was a pioneer. Along with water, the municipal authority also put itself in control of gas, with remarkable results in provision and price. The nineteenth century American journalist Albert Shaw was clearly impressed, "In the rather gloomy winter climate of Glasgow, which necessitates a large use of artificial light, cheap gas in all the tenements however humble, and in every passageway, is an inestimable blessing … No other city in the world, at least outside of Scotland, can at all compare with Glasgow in the universality of the use of gas in the homes of the working classes."

Housing was soon to follow. Twenty years after the clearances of the 1866 Improvement Act, slum life still persisted. The Council decided it could no longer wait for private investment, and constructed hundreds of municipal tenements and business premises across Glasgow. To help the residents of these new dwellings reach their places of work, the city turned its attention to the tramway system, wresting control of the service from commercial business to offer cheaper fares, more convenient routes, and even a healthier operating profit. Shaw again saw fit to comment, hailing it "the best surface transit system in Great Britain".

By the turn of the century, along with water, gas, housing and public transport, Glasgow city owned museums, galleries, schools, libraries, parks, baths, warehouses, shops, halls, churches, a thousand-acre farm, a golf course, a telephone service and the local electricity supply. This was the municipal model in full flow, a reinvention of the very nature of urban existence, and it transfixed and terrified social commentators in equal measures. Was it ancient Athens for the industrial world, a city and its people as one interdependent organism, where, in the words of the *Municipal Reformer,* "men will learn to bear each other's burdens, to care for and protect each other in ways as yet unknown; and citizenship will be a perennial joy"? Or, as *The Times* felt impelled to comment, would it convert "a free city, where every man has liberty to carry on his occupation or his industry under the protection of his local ruler, into a communistic society where those rulers would have all industries under their own control, and deprive him alike of any opportunity for independent enterprise and of any incentive to individual exertion"?

Nearly half a century before, beneath a pewter sky on a Highland loch, Queen Victoria could hardly have guessed the impact of pulling a simple lever. Along with the torrents of water, an ideological choice was sent rushing towards the city.

Improvement had become a political battleground.

PREVIOUS PAGES
Commissioners of the Water Committee of the Loch Katrine Works stand proudly before the tunnel-mouth of the reservoir's great aqueduct. "Among the works, both ancient and modern, for the supply of water to the large cities of the world", wrote the Glasgow Water Works Office in an album produced to commemorate the vast project, "it is acknowledged to hold a prominent place, both as regards the purity of the water, the large quantity available, and the small cost at which it is delivered to the inhabitants".
THOMAS ANNAN 1876 DP025476

RIGHT
At a banquet given in 1860 for Chief Engineer John Frederic Bateman, the guest of honour spoke of the enduring legacy he envisioned for his construction. "I leave you a work which … is as indestructible as the hills through which it has been carried – a truly Roman work, not executed, like the colossal monuments of the East, by forced labour, at the command of an arbitrary sovereign; but by the free will and contributions of a highly civilized and enlightened city, and by the free labour of a free country. It is a work which surpasses the greatest of the nine famous aqueducts which fed the city of Rome; and amongst the works of ornament or usefulness for which your city is now distinguished, and will hereafter be famous, none will be counted more creditable to your wisdom, more worthy of your liberality, or more beneficial in its results, than the Loch Katrine Water Works."
THOMAS ANNAN 1876 CLOCKWISE FROM TOP LEFT DP077627, DP077628, DP077629, DP077630, DP076054 & DP076053

TOP LEFT

Designed by Walter Ralph Herring for the Edinburgh and Leith Corporations' Gas Commission, the construction of Granton Gasworks began in 1898 on land bought from the Duke of Buccleuch. On completion, Granton was the biggest single gas-producing unit in Scotland.

1899 DP074355

CENTRE LEFT, BOTTOM LEFT AND ABOVE
From the giant, iconic cylinders of the Lancashire steam boilers to the arched iron superstructure of the works roof, Granton was typical of the confident civic construction projects pioneered by city authorities to sustain and support their vast new urban environments. By the late nineteenth century, millions of people throughout Britain received their most essential utilities under the supervision of the municipality. It cleaned them, fed them, illuminated their home and street, and carried them to their place of work. For Joseph Chamberlain, the Birmingham industrialist and reformer, this 'gas and water socialism' was the vanguard of a new kind of local governance – municipality with the capacity to transform the city and change people's lives for the better. "By its means you will be able to increase their comforts, to secure their health, to multiply the luxuries which they may enjoy in common, to carry out a vast co-operation system for mutual aid and support, to lessen the inequalities of our social system and to raise the standard of all classes in the community."

1899–1900 DP074354, DP074356 & DP052704

Surrounded by demolition rubble, William Adam's elegant facade is all that remains of Edinburgh's first Royal Infirmary building. Constructed in 1741 on the present day site of Infirmary Street in the Old Town, by the late nineteenth century advances in medical science and a growing population necessitated a move to David Bryce's new, custom-built hospital on Lauriston Place.
1884 SC1173466

Work nears completion on the University of Edinburgh Medical School at Teviot Place, a grand, Venetian-style edifice built around an interior courtyard. Constructed between 1887 and 1889 to a design by Robert Rowand Anderson, a giant tower in the style of St Mark's of Venice was planned for its east end – ultimately only a base with an arched doorway was actually completed.
c1889 DP074901

Behind tall, wrought-iron gates facing Parliamentary Road, the great Glasgow City Poorhouse rises up at once stately and ominous. Originally built as a lunatic asylum in 1809, it was converted to a Victorian poorhouse with space for over 1,500 beds – making it one of the largest social welfare institutions in Britain.
THOMAS ANNAN c1880 DP077229

A huge, neo-gothic chateau sprawling over
Edinburgh's Craiglockhart Hill, Craighouse
Asylum opened in 1894 as the largest, most
progressive asylum of its kind, providing a range
of diverse therapies and environments to stimulate
recovery from mental disorders. Catering exclusively for private, paying patients, it was designed
to recreate the luxurious atmosphere – inside and
out – of a fashionable hydropathic hotel.
H BEDFORD LEMERE 1895 SC701969

Beneath the magnificent, barrel-vaulted ceiling
of the asylum's grand baronial hall, orchestral
recitals and theatre productions were regularly
performed – often by the patients themselves.
The opulent surroundings and furnishings were
intended as an architectural balm, a soothing
and reassuring simulation of the great Victorian
country house for the wealthy and aristocratic
residents of Craighouse.

H BEDFORD LEMERE 1895 SC701974

TOP LEFT

The tiny figure of a janitor in a frock-coat and peaked-cap stands dwarfed by the crisp, new Bruntsfield Primary School building in Edinburgh. Opened in 1895, it was designed in a Scottish renaissance style by Robert Wilson, architect to the Edinburgh School Board.

H BEDFORD LEMERE 1895 SC683632

The School Board encouraged the inclusion of physical exercise in the curriculum, considering it beneficial for discipline, and key to the prized Victorian values of 'a healthy mind and a healthy body'. Bruntsfield's swimming pool and gymnasium were essential parts of the school's institutional machine, an educational factory moulding the children of the Empire. H BEDFORD LEMERE 1895 SC683638 & SC683637

In the classroom of Bruntsfield Primary, desks for over 80 pupils could fold up in single units, with slots designed to hold writing slates. The room was heated by an open fire with – of course – the teacher's desk positioned closest to the hearth. The Victorians invented the concept of education as we understand it today, establishing the tenets – which now seem self-evident – that learning be formalised, education be institutionalised, and imparting knowledge be the duty of society and the state to every citizen. In 1872, primary education was made compulsory for all Scottish children between the ages of five and thirteen.

H BEDFORD LEMERE 1895 SC683634

Teachers and scholars of Oban Sunday School line up for a group photograph during an outing to Crinan. Although there is some debate concerning the origins of Sunday Schools, Robert Raikes, the editor and proprietor of the *Gloucester Journal* is widely credited with – if not their invention – then at the very least their widespread promotion in the late eighteenth century. They became increasingly popular in the Victorian era, prized for their role in instructing future generations in the virtues of faith, self-discipline, industry, thrift and improvement.

J B MACKENZIE c1870 DP075624

RIGHT BELOW

In 1877, Lady Ishbel Maria Hamilton-Gordon, Marchioness of Aberdeen and Temair set about establishing self improvement clubs and societies for the servants of her households and for her husband's tenantry. Committed to promoting the "material, mental and moral elevation of women", Lady Aberdeen expanded her scheme by founding the Haddo House Association for the benefit of Aberdeenshire women farm workers. With over 9,000 members enrolled, it became known as the 'Onward and Upward Association' – also the title of the monthly journal founded and edited by Lady Aberdeen to promote her philanthropic works. Here the women of the Turriff branch arrange themselves for a group photograph.

J B MACKENZIE c1890 DP071945

ABOVE
Sitting on Gilmorehill above the River Kelvin, the gothic edifice of George Gilbert Scott's Glasgow University is a masterpiece of Victorian medievalism. Completed in 1886, the design paid direct homage to the civil architecture found in what Scott called "the ancient seats of industry and commerce in Flanders and Germany".
THOMAS POLSON LUGTON c1900 SC382175

RIGHT
Beneath a barrel-vaulted ceiling supported by rows of tall columns, the busts of past academics and professors stare out across the imposing neo-classical expanse of the University of Edinburgh's Playfair Hall.
SCOTTISH COLORFOTO COLLECTION
c1900 SC1167610

LEFT

Artefacts, specimen jars and assorted curiosities line the shelves of an unidentified anatomy museum.

H BEDFORD LEMERE c1900   SC1138369

TOP RIGHT

Many of the public libraries built in Scotland in the late nineteenth century were partly or wholly financed by the great philanthropist Andrew Carnegie. Featuring an elaborately turreted clocktower, the construction of Peterhead's renaissance-inspired granite library was only possible after Carnegie gifted £1,000 to the local authority in 1890.

c1890   DP073565

BOTTOM RIGHT

Light floods through a domed ceiling on to the reading desks of the Edinburgh Central Library's reference room. Opened in 1890 with a collection of 75,000 books, George Washington Browne's vision for the capital's first truly public library adopted the stylish, humanist architecture of the early French renaissance.

H BEDFORD LEMERE 1893   SC684030

A colossal temple dominated by two dome-capped towers of differing heights, Paisley's Town Hall was the product of an architectural contest between two rival textile magnates. Constructed between 1879 and 1882 to a design by the Belfast architect W H Lynn, the staggeringly grand Town Hall was funded by George A Clark, the owner of the local Anchor thread mill. The building was a response to Clark's great rival, Sir Peter Coats of J & P Coats threadmakers, who in 1870 had funded the construction of the neo-classical Paisley Museum and Library, the first municipal museum in Scotland.

c1882 SC1165239

ABOVE AND RIGHT

Eventually completed in 1897 – 23 years after it was first designed – McEwan Hall's Italianate grandeur is the stone crown at the centre of Edinburgh's university quarter. The construction of the Hall was funded by Sir William McEwan, founder of the Edinburgh brewing firm, Member of Parliament for Central Edinburgh, connoisseur of art and noted philanthropist. Wealthy benefactors played a major role in shaping the character of the Victorian city – they financed many great buildings and monuments that glorified the civic environment, and at the same time embedded their famous names in the everyday fabric of their cities' lives.

SCOTTISH COLORFOTO COLLECTION
c1900 SC11669307

H BEDFORD LEMERE c1897 SC683613

LEFT AND ABOVE
Opened by Queen Victoria in 1888, Glasgow's City Chambers formed the ultimate municipal temple – a monolithic icon of civic wealth, power and dignity that, as Lord Provost Ure proclaimed when laying the building's foundation stone in 1883, was "the citizen's own, to be bought with their money, to be dedicated exclusively to their uses, to pass under their executive control". With domed cupolas at every corner and a dramatically solid central tower, the monumental, Venetian-styled facade is matched and even surpassed by a sumptuous interior of glowing galleries, marble staircases and lavish mosaics. This was architecture by the people, for the people, a statement in stone of the municipal ideal, and an example, as the author James Hamilton Muir wrote in 1901, of "the modern city reverting in importance to the position of the city state in classical antiquity".

LEFT, CLOCKWISE FROM TOP LEFT
H BEDFORD LEMERE c1890 SC1124473, SC1124483, SC1124474 & SC1124476
ABOVE THOMAS POLSON LUGTON c1900 SC1115553

The Collectors

In 1845, a veritable 'who's who' of Victorian high society – including the Duke of Devonshire, the Duchess of Bedford, England's richest heiress Angela Burdett-Coutts, and even Her Majesty the Queen – made up the 120 subscribers to receive the only copies of a startling new book. The novelty of the publication was such that its author felt compelled to include an explanatory "Notice to the Reader" inside each title page: "The plates of the present work are impressed by the agency of light alone, without any aid whatever from the artist's pencil. They are the sun-pictures themselves, and not, as some persons have imagined, engravings in imitation." What followed were 23 calotype pictures – 'calotype' literally meaning 'beautiful image' in Greek – inspired by the life and writings of Sir Walter Scott, which ranged from evocative views of Abbotsford House and Melrose Abbey, to stunning vistas of Loch Katrine and the Trossachs. Entitled *Sun Pictures in Scotland*, this one-guinea book – the first commercially produced collection of landscape photography ever published – was the work of William Henry Fox Talbot, a mathematician, intellectual, gentleman farmer, amateur scientist, and the man who established the foundations of modern photography.

In 1833, Talbot, an aspirant artist, had taken with him on his honeymoon to Lake Como in Italy a 'camera lucida' – a prism used by painters to help them more accurately view scenes. Exasperated with the results of his artworks – he described his sketches as "melancholy to behold" when compared to the visions cast by his artist's aid – he resolved to find a way "to cause these natural images to imprint themselves durably and remain fixed on paper". Remarkably, in 1841, after years of experimentation, Talbot patented the very means of achieving this result. By soaking paper in a combination of common salt and silver nitrate, he discovered that it could become sufficiently light-sensitive to capture and retain an image – it could, in essence, become a photograph.

While continuing to refine this process, in 1844 Talbot published his first book – *The Pencil of Nature* – a visual prospectus outlining the unique potential of his revolutionary discovery. With its eclectic images, which covered everything from architecture and sculpture to botanic studies of natural objects, Talbot's seminal work almost at once created many of the key genres that would dominate photography throughout the coming centuries. *Sun Pictures in Scotland* was his next logical step – a deliberately commercial narrowing of focus that attempted to play to the mid-Victorian vogue for all things Scottish, while at the same time acting as the original template for that soon to be ubiquitous keepsake: the holiday album. Where Talbot led, many in Scotland soon followed. The artist David Octavius Hill had already experimented with the calotype process, which was not protected by patent north of the border, and by the 1850s a new breed of photographer – the amateur enthusiast – was passionately pursuing the medium. Men like the wealthy Aberdonian flour miller John Forbes White, or the fabric printer William Donaldson

Clark were followed by James Bannatyne Mackenzie – Colonsay's first resident minister – and Erskine Beveridge, a Dunfermline linen merchant and earnest antiquarian: their disparate endeavours to record portraits, architecture and archaeology all joined in photography's new, democratic republic.

Photography was one of the most appropriately Victorian of inventions. The era's rigorous obsession with ordering, labelling – and ultimately collecting – the world, ranged across almost every aspect of society. There was a drive both to understand and control the opportunities and challenges created by the huge advancements made in science, technology and industry, and also to master the great truths of the history of man and existence: everything that had led on to the 'pinnacle' of the Victorian age. To that end, the seemingly cool, dispassionate eye of the camera became a cherished assistant: trustworthy, exacting and relentless. This was certainly the view of Lady Elizabeth Eastlake, the author and art critic, who in 1857 in *The Quarterly Review* wrote of photography as being "made for the present age … the sworn witness of everything presented to her view. What are her unerring records in the service of mechanics, engineering, geology, and natural history, but facts of the most sterling and stubborn kind?"

While the photograph was emerging as the ultimate tool for description and analysis on both an individual and a mass scale, the new institutions arising to cater for the era's increasing public thirst for knowledge faced an even greater 'collecting' task. For the great Victorian museum, the goal was not to capture likenesses – however exact – but to amass and assemble the definite articles. The success of the Great Exhibition of 1851 had in many ways transformed the popular appreciation of art and artefacts – not least by introducing the prospect of incredible scale and spectacle to the experience. Although this spread disquiet among some higher echelons of society – who saw cultural environments as the province of the elite – for the progressive reformers, enlightenment through exhibitions was the first step towards an idealised civil society. "The first function of a museum", wrote the art critic and social thinker John Ruskin in 1880, "is to give example of perfect order and perfect elegance in the true sense of that test word, to the disorderly and rude populace". Backed by an enthusiastic Prince Albert, museums began to emerge as new civic landmarks, their essentially egalitarian, educational purpose often the vehicle for monolithic displays of imperial wealth and power – carrying the implicit message that, if national treasures and natural history were to be on public show, then no one would surpass the holdings of the British Empire.

162.

Oratory at Kilneuair, Lochawe.

Born in December 1833 on St Kilda – the so-called island at the end of the world – James Bannatyne Mackenzie was a son of the manse of Kilbrandon in Argyll, and would follow in his father's footsteps to become the first resident minister on the island of Colonsay. He used his camera to record West Highland gravestones, as well as creating more sentimental and artistic photographs. Here he captures a figure relaxing among the ruins of St Columba's Chapel at Kilneuair, Loch Awe.

J B MACKENZIE c1870 SC1063855

Keills N.º 1 Ancient Chapel.

A study of two backs – a smartly dressed man rests his head against the Keills Cross. Both the man's face and the sculpture's intricate frontage remain out of sight as they look down to the ruined chapel by Loch Na Cille's shoreline. An artistic sensibility and awareness of the story-telling power of the camera elevates J B Mackenzie's work above many other early practitioners. Shortly after taking this photograph, Mackenzie had to process the glass plate negative in his small portable dark room tent – visible here in the centre left of the picture – working with noxious chemicals and potentially dangerous ether fumes to secure the image for his collection.

J B MACKENZIE c1870 DP058936

In 1895, at Pun Brae, Stevenston, Ayrshire, a Bronze Age burial cist was discovered while digging the foundations of a building. Standing outside a dilapidated cottage, the barefoot children are as fascinated by the photographer as they are by the cist. Road improvements and construction work regularly uncovered long hidden remnants from the distant past. By capturing this scene, local photographer Samuel Beckett has created an important visual record of the cist before its ultimate destruction in the name of progress.

SAMUEL BECKETT 1895 SC589880

John Nicolson was a Caithness farmer with a passion for the past. He actively collected historic and archaeological artefacts and assembled a wealth of knowledge about the archaeology and history of the county. When the former MP and diplomat Sir Francis Tress Barry purchased Keiss Castle in 1890, Nicolson undertook a number of archaeological excavations of brochs for Barry. But Nicolson was also a talented artist and sculptor and used his skills to record in watercolour many of the excavated objects. Pictured here in the garden of his house at Summerbank in Nybster, Caithness, Nicolson – second from the right – is surrounded by his family, his sculptures and a range of discovered artefacts.

c1885 SC1172768

This diver on the pier at Dalerb, Loch Tay, may well have been exploring the offshore island and priory. The technology of marine exploration was in its infancy, and often encountered teething problems. The Reverend Odo Blundell recounted his less than successful attempt at exploring Loch Ness in 12ft of water "owing to the inexperience of the amateurs at the airpump, little serious work was done. The excess of air which was supplied to me had the effect of making me so buoyant that I was floating over the tops of the stones instead of stepping firmly on them, and that despite the two lead weights of 56lbs each attached to the already very heavy helmet and boots."

J B MACKENZIE c1890 DP075653

The Victorian quest for knowledge and understanding of the past saw the Society of Antiquaries of Scotland undertaking a number of archaeological excavations on Roman sites in the final years of the century. Some of the most impressive remains – including the multiple upstanding ramparts of a fort dating from the second century AD – were discovered here at Ardoch. Excavations were led by Mr J H Cunningham – seated left – a civil engineer and Treasurer of the Society.

1896–97 DP074897

The Ordnance Survey undertook detailed surveys across the UK in the nineteenth century, beginning in Scotland in 1843–44 in the counties of Wigtown and Kirkcudbright. Six inches to the mile was the scale selected to provide uniform coverage of the whole of the country, and the exquisitely produced first edition maps contained a wealth of detail and information about the landscape. Accurate measurements and the skills of the surveyor were also essential for building projects or for improvements to the roads and railways. The identity of the picutred survey team is unknown.

c1870 DP073841

In 1866 William Donaldson Clark gave a presentation to the Edinburgh Photographic Society on his recent work at Melrose Abbey. With his friend John Smith of Darnick, he had taken identical photographs of the abbey using different lenses and concluded that the new lens from the camera-maker Mr Dallmeyer gave the best possible pictures. Clark erected scaffolding to achieve a comprehensive survey of the Abbey, on occasion introducing figures – as here – to add to the sentimental impact of the photograph.

John Forbes White once commented that his photographs "entailed the hardest work of his life", and his biographer I M Harrower notes that "sometimes irate hotel-keepers would ask him to remove himself and his obnoxious chemicals". An art collector and miller by profession, White was an amateur photographer for only a few years in the late 1850s, producing some enduring images of Scottish architecture and landscapes, as here at St Magnus Cathedral, Kirkwall.

Many of William Donaldson Clark's photographs were shown at the exhibitions of the Photographic Society of Scotland. He captured the changing face of Edinburgh, from new buildings like the National Gallery in 1858, to more historic parts of the city, as well as beautiful landscape shots. In this atmospheric scene at Melrose Abbey, the man in the photograph may well be Donaldson Clark himself.

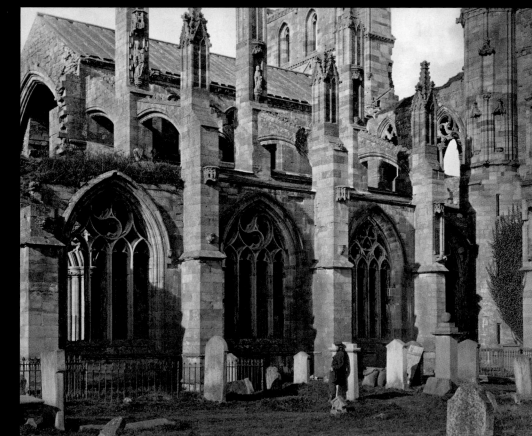

Camera records camera during what may be a photographic society outing, as an interested group stands between the two bulky pieces of equipment – one part of the scene, the other capturing it – in the grounds of Dunfermline Abbey. Clubs and societies grew in popularity, and meetings of people interested in the developing art of photography occurred regularly in the years after its invention. Societies offered the opportunity to share knowledge and experiences with others through lectures, demonstrations and excursions.

c1890 SC381288

In 1884, the proprietor of *The Scotsman*, John Ritchie Findlay, generously gifted to Scotland a sum of £50,000 for a new building to house the Scottish National Portrait Gallery and the National Museum of Antiquities, "a treasure house of the industrial progress of Scotland, and of the men and women who made her famous". Based in Edinburgh, the Portrait Gallery or 'Scottish Valhalla', contained portraits of Scottish authors, poets and royalty, as well as engravings, busts, some statuary and a collection of medallion portraits, as here in the first-floor gallery.
H BEDFORD LEMERE c1900 SC466067

BELOW RIGHT

Designed by Sir Robert Rowand Anderson, the Portrait Gallery opened in July 1889, with the Museum of Antiquities following two years later. The decoration of the "great Gothic palace" included a frieze of Scottish historical figures around the balcony walls of the entrance hall.
H BEDFORD LEMERE c1900 SC684146

OPPOSITE

At the first meeting of the Society of Antiquaries of Scotland to be held in the library of the new museum in Queen Street, the Marquis of Bute expressed appreciation at the generosity of J R Findlay who had "recognised that although archaeology was the study of the dead past, it was not the mere indulgence of an idle, though intelligent, curiosity. As was anatomy to physiology and to medicine, so was archaeology to the history and the life of the present and the future." As was typical of the time, displays in the new National Museum of Antiquities were very crowded, with an emphasis on quantities of similar objects grouped together to allow comparisons.
H BEDFORD LEMERE c1900 SC684147

When Charles Darwin was a student
in Edinburgh in 1825, the University
Medical School had the finest natural
history museum in Britain. The founder,
Dr Alexander Monro *Secundus*, pre-
sented his own anatomical collection,
as well as his father's, to the University.
Many valuable additions followed and
a three-storeyed, galleried museum
was incorporated into the new Medical
School on Teviot Place. Here the bust
of Dr Monro stares out from a startling
arrangement of the skulls and skeletons of
elephants, hippopotamuses, chimpanzees
and ceiling-hung dolphins and whales.

H BEDFORD LEMERE 1895 SC694690

Wonderland

On 12 December 1881, the steamship SS *Surania,* inbound from New York, completed its Atlantic crossing to dock at Broomielaw in Glasgow. A crowd of hundreds, by turns expectant and sceptical, milled on the quayside, eager to see the unloading of what was reputed to be an exceptional cargo. This uncertain, excited buzz was the work of Thomas Lipton – grocer, salesman, PR pioneer, tea-merchant, yachtsman and one of Clydeside's most famous and successful sons. The press had already been primed with an array of fantastical statistics. Stowed in the hold were two enormous cheeses, each weighing 3,472 pounds, churned and set by Dr L L Wright of Whitesboro, the head of America's largest dairy. Lipton claimed 200 dairy maids had milked 800 cows for six days to produce the 4,000 gallons of milk required to create the 2ft thick, 11ft wide giants.

From the Broomielaw docks, the cheeses went their separate ways. One was taken by train to the Universal Cookery and Food Exhibition at the Royal Aquarium, Westminster, and the other – known as Jumbo, after a famed P T Barnum elephant – was pulled through Glasgow by traction engine to Lipton's flagship store on the High Street. Whether by accident or design – it was never clear with Lipton's publicity stunts – Jumbo was too big to fit through the front door. Fortunately, the Jamaica Street branch had a wider entrance, and the cheese was eventually heaved into position in the store's front window.

But Lipton was not finished yet, as he recalled in his memoirs, *Leaves from the Lipton Logs.* "Why not make the Giant Cheese a better advertisement still by turning it into a Golden Cheese by the simple method of hiding a large quantity of sovereigns or half-sovereigns in its vast interior?" On Christmas Eve, Lipton, decked out in his trademark white suit and apron and flanked by a dozen police officers, stood astride his cheese, carving off hunks for customers, who instantly tore aside the wrapping in a desperate search for the hidden coins. "The newspaper reporters", he remarked, "came along in force and next morning I had columns of free publicity."

The entrepreneurs of the nineteenth century had learnt fast. The appetites of the common man for both sensation and consumption were growing at an incredible rate. When brought together by showmen like Lipton, the thrill seeking, shopaholic Victorians found the mix heady, intoxicating and near irresistible.

What can sometimes get lost amidst the visions of raw, muscular power that characterise the industrial revolution is that the legendary scale, the great feats of technological advancement, were a means to an end. The one overriding, inevitable consequence of living in the greatest manufacturing society the world had ever known was the unrelentling, endless production of *things*. Ever-more products. Ever-more choice.

Lipton was a key figure in the promotion of the concept of 'the necessities'. His shops stocked limited ranges of goods – bacon, ham, butter, eggs and, of course, cheese – but in huge quantities, and he aimed directly at the mass market, with stores either in high streets or in smaller streets in densely populated working-class neighbourhoods. His Glasgow shops alone, he boasted, daily sold a ton and a half of 'lumpy' butter, 50 cases of 'roll' butter, a ton of bacon, a ton and a half of ham, half a ton of cheese, and 16,000 eggs.

Lipton's business model for expansion was to recreate this format wherever he could – same products, different places, more customers. As his grocery empire moved into England, adverts began to appear in the newspapers of the cities he targeted. Plain and unadorned, their simple message comprised just three words: "Lipton is Coming".

While chains of convenience stores started to proliferate across Britain, others took a different approach. Their goal was not expansion by outlets, but by the range of goods and services a single store could offer. This was the ambition of Charles Jenner and Charles Kennington, who had first taken the lease of 47 Princes Street in Edinburgh in 1838, with the intention of providing the people of the capital with the finest silks and linens. By the end of the century – and despite a destructive fire in 1892 – 'Jenner's' had subsumed the surrounding properties to become the largest shop in Scotland. Except it was more than just a shop. Here was a consumer wonderland, an endless array of objects under one roof, the luxury bazaar Emile Zola called "The Ladies' Paradise" – the department store. Luring customers from the street with the new phenomenon of the window display, inside waited mazes of counters festooned with ribbons, lace, gloves and jewellery, corridor after corridor of the finest furniture and ornaments, hydraulic lifts and lavish electrical lighting, a kaleidoscope of colour, consumerism and desire: shopping as entertainment.

In the nineteenth century, a whole society had stepped through the looking glass. The children of the industrial revolution were the creators of the culture of leisure and pleasure for the masses. If you weren't happy with your life, you could buy a new one, find it in the fineries of the latest clothing, lose yourself in the pages of a sensational novel or the passion of a sporting contest, alter your mind with over-the-counter drugs from your local Chemist. The list of popular innovations that can be attributed to the Victorians is as eclectic as it is surprising. They gave us product placement, junk mail, Christmas crackers, the football league, fish and chips, interior design, and the scoop newspaper story. They invented the theme park, the movies, the amusement arcade, crime fiction, heated curling tongs, vending machines and the shopping mall. Above all, for better or for worse, the Victorians invented us.

ABOVE AND RIGHT

Two proprietors stand waiting earnestly for custom. A & D Padon opened in Edinburgh's St Andrew Square in 1853, specialising in selling account books to nearby financial institutions. For Thomas Smail, a Jedburgh printer, stationer and bookseller, the goal was to tailor his business to cater to the developing tourism market. The opening of a railway line to the historic Borders town in 1860 had brought the steady influx of the day-tripper. Amongst other publications, Smail produced a *Borders Map* and a *Guide to Jedburgh*, and sold prints by professional photographers like George Washington Wilson, advertising them prominently in his shop front displays.

c1890 DP073846 & DP071938

The Royal Polytechnic Warehouse opened on Glasgow's Jamaica Street in 1867 as one of the finest shopping institutions in the city, selling drapery, haberdashery and fancy wares. As James Hamilton Muir recognised in *Glasgow in 1901*, Jamaica Street and the intersecting Argyle Street were commercial hubs: "Here business cracks her stoutest whip, and men move fast and silently and work very late. Every species of merchandise, from twopenny watches to cargoes of sugar, is sold in this district, and the buyers and sellers are ever on the pavement."

THOMAS ANNAN c1880 DP074851

"A mile of commercial palaces" was how Robert Louis Stevenson described Edinburgh's Princes Street in 1879, with its drapers, bazaars, jewellers, perfumers, fruiterers and shoe shops. Charles Kennington and Charles Jenner first opened a store here in 1838 in converted houses, but after fire destroyed the premises in 1892, a new, purpose-built wonderland emerged from the devastation. Designed by William Hamilton Beattie, the building's scale, grandeur and attention to detail aimed to impress. Jenner died in 1893, before he could see the store reopen, but a codicil in his will bequeathed £8,000 towards external decoration. A series of caryatides – female figures carved into columns – were added to the intricate facade, intended as symbolic representations of women as the supporters of the business.

H BEDFORD LEMERE 1895 SC678398

Writing to her mother at the end of the nineteenth century, the Crown Princess of Greece expressed the feverish excitement of the shopaholic after a visit to London's great commercial emporiums: "We spent I don't know how many hours at Maple & Liberty! I screamed at the things ... but they were too lovely! *No*, these shops I go mad in them! I would be ruined if I lived here longer!" The new breed of shops sold not just an array of delightful goods, but also an experience – a taste of luxury and the seductive joy of the purchase – to the masses. The reopened Jenner's styled itself as Scotland's commercial palace *par excellence*: grand, opulent and enticing, with more objects on display than its customers even knew existed, let alone wanted. On 4 December 1895, an advertisement appeared in *The Scotsman* for Jenner's "Great National Bazaar and Christmas Fancy Fair". There were goods from India, China and Japan, their "remarkable feature" being "the moderate price at which such beautiful and useful articles can be purchased". There were "many typical examples of the inventive genius of Americans" and of "the artistic talents of France and Austria ... strikingly illustrated by the number of novelties from Paris and Vienna". And from Germany, and the factories of Nuremberg and Sonneberg, "an object-lesson of the amazing amount of care and thought expended in the production of toys and dolls, to delight the juvenile mind".

OPPOSITE, LEFT TO RIGHT FROM TOP
H BEDFORD LEMERE 1895 SC678376, SC678391, SC466078, SC678395, SC678383 & SC678370
LEFT FROM TOP H BEDFORD LEMERE 1895
SC678389 & SC678369

TOP LEFT, BOTTOM LEFT AND ABOVE

"Glasgow, in truth, is a very Tokio for tea-rooms", reported the book *Glasgow in 1901*. "Nowhere can one have so much for so little, and nowhere are such places more popular and frequented." Miss Cranston's Tea Rooms opened on Buchanan Street in 1897, the quirky yet stylish ambience scoring an instant hit with the people of the city. At

a time when the temperance movement was increasingly influential, tea-rooms provided a convivial environment for Glaswegians from all walks of life to gather and enjoy non-alcoholic drinks. Spread over five floors, George Walton's Arts and Crafts interiors and furnishings – with intricate murals by Charles Rennie

Mackintosh – created an avant-garde complex of tea and luncheon rooms, smoking and billiards rooms for men, and 'ladies only' facilities where 'respectable' women could meet.

CLOCKWISE FROM TOP LEFT

H BEDFORD LEMERE 1897 SC702109,

SC702106 & SC702107

ABOVE

Cricketers assume exaggerated poses in this carefully staged group shot of an unidentified club – the photograph annotated only with the initials 'ACC'. Cricket was once a very popular sport in Scotland, before the advent of football. At a time when health and fitness were held up as ideal Victorian virtues, sports clubs – usually exclusively male – provided the opportunity for social interaction, as well as promoting physical well-being.

1868 DP028983

TOP RIGHT

Played with wrought iron hoops thrown at a pin some 22 yards distant, quoiting was an extremely popular working man's sport, with interest in matches regularly heightened by laying on wagers. Here at St Fort in Fife, the presence of pipers suggests a competition in progress.

1893–96 DP007392

BOTTOM RIGHT

Standing by their stones, with backs to the camera, the men of the St Fort Curling Club raise their brushes in mock salute. Curling is thought to have been invented in late medieval Scotland, with the first written reference to a contest using stones on ice coming from the records of Paisley Abbey in Renfrewshire in February 1541.

1895 SC979646

JEDBURGH GAMES (BICYCLISTS) 1887. A.R.E.

The gentlemen of the Stanley Cycling Club stand confidently beside their bicycles. The invention of the safety bicycle in the 1880s replaced the incredibly challenging penny farthing, and cycling soon emerged as a popular recreational pastime, providing a wonderfully novel way of exploring the countryside.

1889 DP070849

BOTTOM LEFT

The five entrants in the '1½ Mile Velocipede Handicap Race' stand ready at the centre of the busy crowd of the Border Games in Jedburgh. Each year, the start of the games was heralded at six o'clock in the morning by the firing of four shots from a cannon, the ringing of church bells and instrumental and flute bands parading through the streets.

ANDREW R EDWARDS 1887 DP071936

ABOVE

A lady golfer addresses the ball in the light rough, just off the rather rocky fairway of a hole at Golspie Golf Club in Sutherland. Founded in 1889, Golspie was one of many new courses opening across Scotland at the end of the nineteenth century. Middle-class women seeking the health benefits of fresh air and exercise were attracted to the decorous pace of the game.

c1900 SC1092507

A shooting party of beaters, ghillies and gentleman hunters pose with their haul at Loch Lomond. In Victorian society, field sports were almost exclusively the recreational domain of the nobility, aristocracy and landed gentry. Huge estates were cultivated as private wildernesses, playgrounds of the elite, with 'Highland safaris' offering the likes of deer stalking, grouse shooting and trout fishing to the select few.

1894 SC939890

The Sun Never Sets

They were billed as the greatest shows on earth. Everything was there to entertain and enthral. Galleries of fine art, industrial invention and engineering marvel competed with displays of interior luxuries and imperial exoticisms. There was Thomson's Patent Gravity Switchback railway, and Signor Balleni in his hot air balloon. You could watch live diamond cutting, a loom that made hygienic woollen underwear, the Power Drop biscuit machine and an Indian fakir on a bed of nails. There was the chance to take a ride on a Venetian gondola, or visit an oriental smoking lounge, a Dutch cocoa house, a Bachelors' Café or the world's largest terracotta fountain. And you were encouraged to stay a while, to linger into the evening, for, as the *Art Journal* recognised, more pleasures lay in store. "By day, with bands playing and well-dressed crowds of promenaders, the scene is one of gaiety and brightness, and when night falls, and the electric light shines brilliantly, and from the fairy fountain the many-coloured waters climb into the sky, the sober-sided citizens of Glasgow can hardly believe that some spirit of enchantment has not transformed their own grey, steady-going town into the likeness of Paris on a fete day."

The Glasgow Exhibitions of 1888 and 1901 were Victorian extravaganzas on the largest scale, showcases of the era that celebrated improvement and innovation and distilled them to their most spectacular and crowd-pleasing. On 8 May 1888, the Prince and Princess of Wales were driven through cheering crowds to open the first Exhibition's centrepiece, an Oriental and Moorish palace designed by the architect James Sellars – dubbed 'Baghdad on Kelvinside'. Since the Great Exhibition of 1851, the trend for enormous spectacle had come to characterise the public entertainments of the Victorians, with the frantic, mass-consumption of novelty emerging as one of the defining qualities of the nineteenth century experience. As a response to Edinburgh's 1886 International Exhibition and Manchester's 1887 Royal Jubilee Exhibition, Glasgow was tasked with meeting increasingly demanding expectations – its events had to be bigger, more exciting and more thrilling, festivals of the incredible, powerful enough to overwhelm the senses.

But for a city pursuing a progressive policy of municipal governance, this was about more than just putting on a fantastical show. All of the wonders of the 1888 Exhibition had been assembled with the express aim of raising money for what was to be Glasgow's crowning glory – the ultimate symbol of transformation and improvement – a permanent, public, palace of art. Profits, topped up with subscriptions from the people of the city, created a building to dominate Kelvingrove Park. Opened to coincide with the launch of the second Exhibition in 1901, the new Art Gallery and Museum was a striking creation in deep-red sandstone, an enormous baroque edifice that drew direct inspiration from Spain's famous pilgrimage church of Santiago de Compostela. With a floor area of almost half a million square feet, and a Fine Arts section housing 2,700 exhibits alone – including paintings by Turner, Constable and Gainsborough – it was designed as an icon of civic pride, a bold statement to the world of Glasgow's great energy and sophistication.

The impetus that lay behind the exhibition craze was that most unshakeable of Victorian traits: self-confidence. There was a widespread, near universal, conviction that their age was the greatest in the history of civilisation – and that it would last forever. The message was clear: Britain was the most advanced technological and industrial nation on earth. For the vast swathes of the globe painted imperial red, a bright, brave future of knowledge and innovation awaited. As Prince Albert himself said in 1850 when launching the first Great Exhibition, "we are living at a period of most wonderful transition, which tends rapidly to accomplish that great end, to which, indeed, all history points – the realisation of the unity of mankind".

Admirable as this utopian sentiment might be, as the century drew to a close, it was clear that history had other ideas. An age of furious progress was ending. The great British Empire was massively over-stretched, and a tipping point was fast approaching. The government of so many by so few could not persist. The Victorians had once set out to model themselves on ancient Rome. Now, the world was remembering that the ultimate destiny of Empire is to fall.

Queen Victoria, the figurehead of the era, died at Osborne House on the Isle of Wight at half past six in the evening on 22 January 1901. Sealed in her casket with a startling array of trinkets and keep-sakes, from rings, bracelets, shawls and lockets, to Prince Albert's dressing-gown and a photo of John Brown, her body was transferred the short distance across the Solent to Portsmouth harbour, en route to Windsor and her requested military funeral. As the *Alberta* made the short sea-voyage with Her Majesty's coffin on board, she passed through an 8 mile-long honour guard of steel, in which the British fleet was joined by foreign warships, each spaced 1,500 feet apart. The imposing grey hulls of *Australia*, *Nile* and *Trafalgar* gave way to the *Dupuy de Lome* of France, the *Dom Carlo I* of Portugal, the *Hatsuse* of Japan, and four giant, imposing ironclads from the country of Victoria's grandson – the Kaiser.

A mournful, somnolent Britain entered the reign of Edward VII. Beyond, gathered the storm clouds of the most terrible conflict the world had ever seen.

In the cathedral-like Machinery and Industrial Halls, muscular totems of engineering might are arranged in vast exhibits of polished iron and steel. The official 1901 Exhibition guidebook encouraged a visitor response of reverence and awe. "The thought will no doubt arise that the machines here exhibited, in this year of grace 1901, have a significance and a power for changing the conditions of labour such as machinery never before possessed. Here, in the germ stages perhaps, are the beginnings of those colossal machines, driven by compressed air and electricity, that will produce extraordinary changes in the history of mankind."

T & R ANNAN & SONS 1901 DP040948

The 1901 site sprawled over 73 acres of Glasgow's Kelvingrove Park, with the proud new Art Gallery and Museum a stunning centrepiece alongside the gloriously extravagant temporary structure of the Eastern Palace. The Exhibition was a truly international wonderland, with visitors afforded the opportunity to visit a village of Russian timber buildings, spend sixpence to slide down a Canadian Water Chute, marvel at feats of juggling in the Indian Theatre, or delight at the music of the Romanian orchestra in a grand, 3,000-seater concert hall.

1901 LEFT TO RIGHT FROM TOP LEFT
DP038987, DP038975, DP038973, DP038974,
DP038986, DP038972, DP038877, DP038971,
DP038982, DP038979 & DP038985

Every night, with great ceremony, the illumination of the Exhibition grounds and the great Eastern Palace would take place. In scale and novelty, these elaborate lightshows made for a breathtaking spectacle, creating the pleasing illusion of some secret, magic kingdom nestling within Glasgow's relentless industrial cityscape.

T & R ANNAN & SONS 1901 DP040966

Swaddled in furs, a woman waits in her carriage outside James Clinkskill's general store in Prince Albert, Canada. The son of a Glasgow iron founder, Clinkskill left home in 1882 at the age of 28, aboard the Allan Line's *Parisian* out of Liverpool. Arriving in Halifax, he travelled by train via Montreal, Toronto and Chicago to Winnipeg. A brief attempt at homesteading convinced him that his future lay elsewhere. "Amongst the active immigration of the early 1880s", wrote Clinkskill in his memoirs, "were some who, not being adapted to farming, decided to try their fortune in catering to the newcomers by establishing trading businesses at points remote from the only railway line, the main line of the Canadian Pacific. Two of these were my partner and myself."

pre1901 DP073848

Passengers en route to the New World stare curiously into the camera lens from the wide deck of the steamship ss *Oregon*. The *Oregon* was a record-breaking passenger liner that won the Blue Riband for the Guion Line – the Liverpool and Great Western Steamship Company that operated the Liverpool / Queenstown / New York route – as the fastest ship on the Atlantic in 1884.

ERSKINE BEVERIDGE 1885 DP042681

ABOVE

The challenge for many emigrants was
to lay down lasting roots in wild, largely
undeveloped frontiers. Burrard Inlet in
Canada is captured here in 1885 by Erskine
Beveridge, the wealthy Dunfermline linen
manufacturer and noted amateur photographer. Having sailed to New York to
monitor his business interests, Beveridge
then travelled extensively around North
America, taking photographs throughout
his journey of locations ranging from
Missouri and Colorado to British
Columbia. Remarkably, this image, which
speaks so strongly of the fragile footholds
being established in the new territories,
is the modern-day site of the great city of
Vancouver.

ERSKINE BEVERIDGE 1885 DP050375

A camel train pauses before the majestic Sphinx and
Pyramids of Giza, with the great paws and body of the
Sphinx still largely buried by sand. These crumbling
remnants of a once great Empire had become a stop
on the international 'grand tour' for wealthy Victorian
travellers. John Cook, son of Thomas, had played a large
part in popularising Egypt as a tourist destination in the
1880s, including opening hotels in Luxor and offering
Nile pleasure cruises in opulent steamships.

pre 1901 DP075267

A strident-looking colonial stands amidst a native settlement in Delagoa Bay, Mozambique. Now known as Maputo – the present-day capital of Mozambique – the inlet had assumed strategic importance for centuries. First explored by the Portuguese in 1544, it was established as a trading post for ivory and slaves, became a way station for frigates making the East India Spice run, and, by the nineteenth century, was prized for its inland routes to the South African diamond mines and goldfields. Ownership of the colony was continually contested between the Portuguese, Dutch, British and the Boers, until it was awarded to Portugal by arbitration in 1875.

B W CANEY c1890 DP077201

TOP LEFT

Botha's Cutting formed part of the railway line that linked Durban to the inland town of Pietermaritzberg and the coalfields of northern Natal in South Africa. Colonial photography was often about the implicit reinforcement of western superiority and progress, drawing on the likes of civil engineering projects and urban developments as evidence of the benefits of British rule.
B W CANEY c1890 DP077206

CENTRE LEFT

Surrounded by tropical foliage, the Jubilee Fountain was built in Durban's Market Square to commemorate 60 years since Victoria's ascension to the throne.
c1899 DP077197

BOTTOM LEFT

Durban's wide West Street is a busy mixture of the familiar and the exotic, its Victorian colonial architecture mixing with the vibrant dynamic of the frontier town. First annexed by British authorities in 1843, over the next half-century Durban developed from a ramshackle trading station of wooden huts and shanties into one of the most important seaports of the Empire.
pre1901 DP077200

RIGHT

Workers toil among the Cape's great fields of sugarcane. A massive boom in the industry in the late nineteenth century saw Durban become the largest trading terminal for sugar in the world.
B W CANEY c1890 DP077203

In the welcome shade of an Indian riverside, a party, with attendant servant, stop for a refined, decorous picnic. Ruled by the Empress Victoria, the subcontinent's alluring exoticisms offered a life and an environment far removed from the smoky, industrial morass of the British homeland. This was the land of Rudyard Kipling, the laureate of imperial India, a place that, in the imaginations of the adventurous, awakened the primitive emotions of curiosity, mystery and romance. Yet, as Kipling wrote in his short story collection *Plain Tales from the Hills,* "India is a place beyond all others where one must not take things too seriously – the midday sun always excepted. Too much work and too much energy kill a man just as effectively as too much assorted vice or too much drink."

pre1901 DP074342

Index